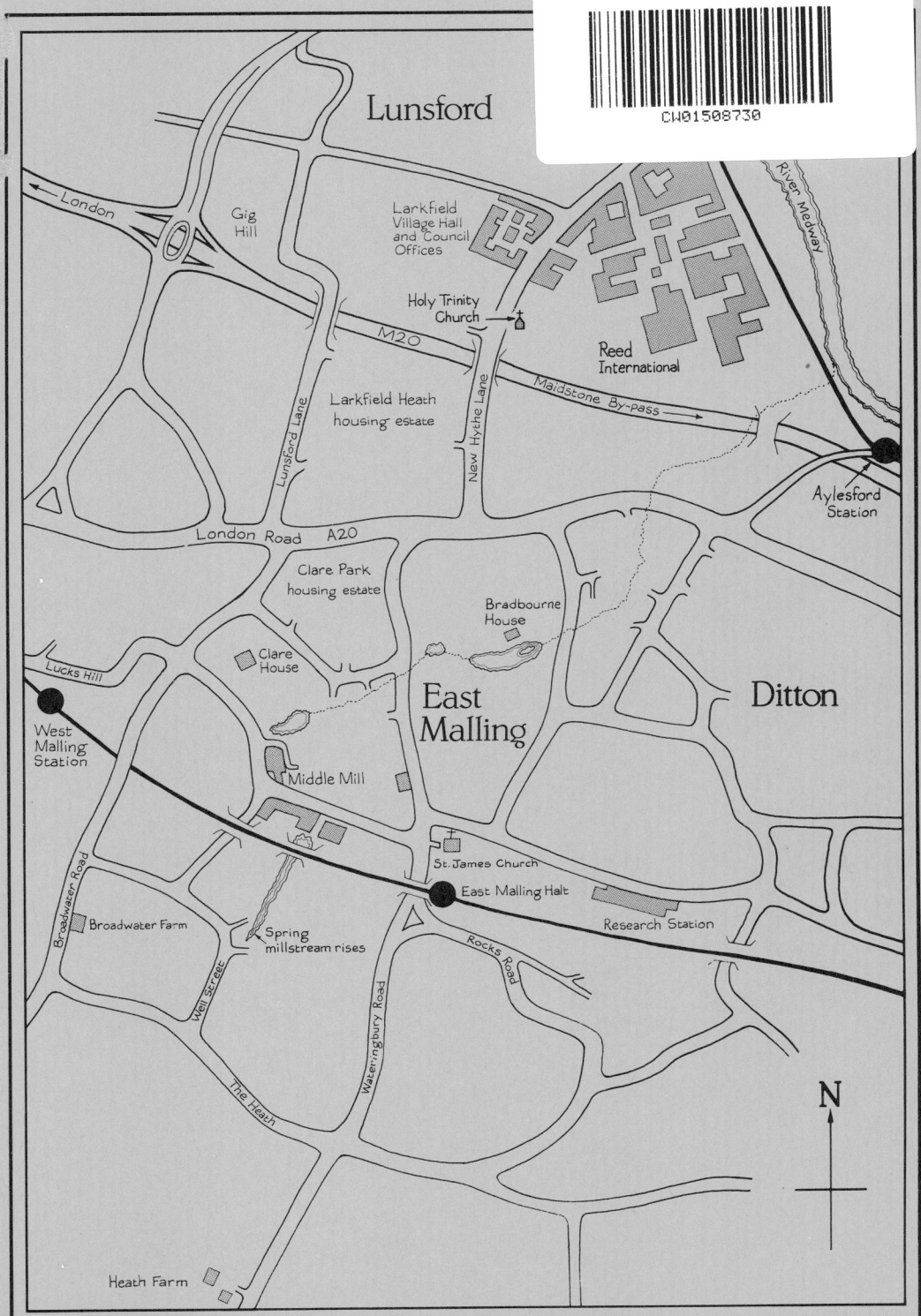

PORTRAIT OF A KENTISH VILLAGE

# PORTRAIT
# OF A
# KENTISH VILLAGE

**East Malling 827–1978**

Michael McNay

LONDON

VICTOR GOLLANCZ LTD

1980

ISBN 0 575 02876 9

In memory of Lindsey Bird

Printed in Great Britain by
Westerham Press

# Contents

# Illustrations

The map below shows the Manor of East Malling as surveyed by
Isaac Gostling in 1706.

*The chapter decorations are taken from* The Book of Maps of the Estate of the Right Worshipful Sir Roger Twisden Bart., *which was produced by Abraham Walter during the 1680s.*

*All are reproduced by courtesy of the Kent County Council Archives.*

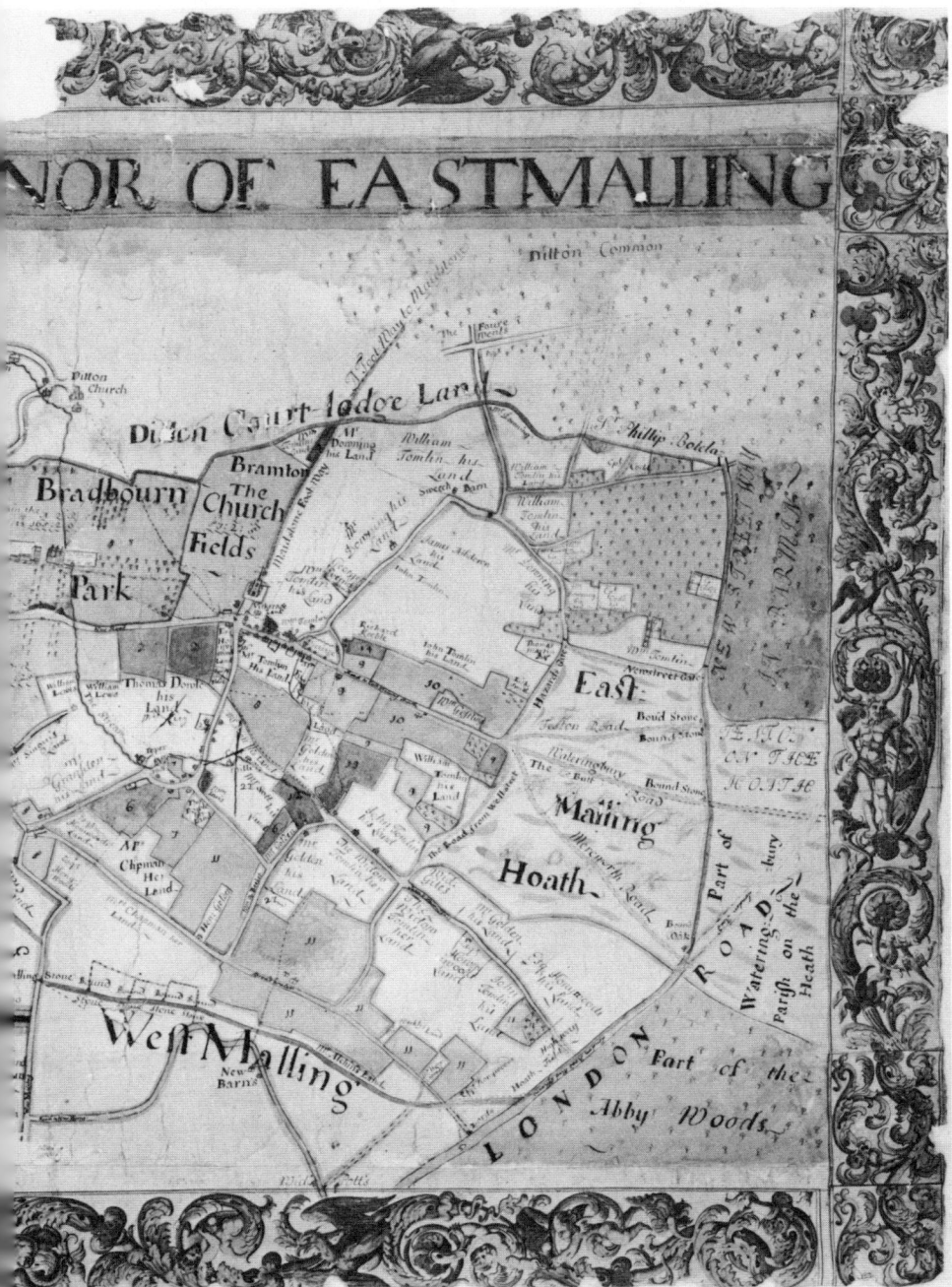

# Preface

There is an irony in a comparative newcomer writing a book about East Malling (pronounced Mawling, naturally; just as near-by Meopham is pronounced Mepum and Wrotham is pronounced Rootum and Trottis-cliffe is pronounced Trosley). As a car-borne daily commuter to Fleet Street I am one of those responsible for the change in the nature of the village. The change is irreversible, but change needs to be controlled and — at any rate before the conservation-conscious last few years — it has not been controlled enough.

Even now, and in spite of the small benefits for rural communities bestowed by the 1972 Local Government Act (see chapter 8), the drift is towards larger units of government making decisions more remote from the people immediately affected. Look at the Channel Tunnel project: it won't, pray God, affect East Malling, but it will affect East Kent and nobody has yet started to think seriously about what that means to life in the area or to the landscape of one of England's most beautiful counties. According to a 1973 issue of *New Scientist*, the Channel Tunnel would have a catastrophic effect on the North Downs, and there would be a twenty-mile-wide swathe of industrial/urban building all the way from Folkestone to Ashford. Now *there* is something that isn't envisaged in the Kent Structure Plan.

Anyway, I hope this book shows that many of the features of present-day village life, with their continuity reaching back to the time of Edward the Confessor and beyond, are worth sympathy. Some things have changed since I wrote the book: there are, for instance, new faces on the council since the elections, but the underlying reality is the same. Wages quoted are 1978 figures.

Apart from the people quoted in the book, I would like to thank Mary Clarke, who planted the idea, and my wife Sue Pilkington, who helped with the research and did the bulk of the typing of the final draft. Professor A. F. Posnette helped far more than appears from the references to him in the book, as did Mr Reg Spice and Messrs John and Richard Mercer. I would also like to thank Mr Stuart Lawrie and Mr David

Stroud of Reed Aylesford and Mrs Eunice Hubbard. Most of the historical material came from the East Malling parish papers and the Twisden family papers in the magnificently run county archive at Maidstone, but I am also heavily indebted to Michael Fuller for his privately published book on the mills of East Malling, to C. L. Sinclair Williams for his article 'Maritime East Malling' in *Archaeologia Cantiana* (1973), and to S. C. Pearce, D. W. Greenham, and B. S. Furneaux for their studies of the land owned by East Malling Research Station. Other sources include *Captain Swing* by E. J. Hobsbawm and George Rudé (1969), Edward Hasted's *History and Topographical Survey of the County of Kent* (1778–99), *The Domesday Book of Kent* by Lambert Larking (1869), the Kent volumes of the *Victoria County History*, *The Family of Twysden and Twisden* by Sir John Ramskill Twisden (1939), and *Puritan's Progress* by Monica Furlong (1975).

*East Malling*                                                                    M. M.
*June 1979*

PORTRAIT OF A KENTISH VILLAGE

...and so away, it being a mighty cold and windy,
but clear day, and had the pleasure of seeing the Medway
running, winding up and down mightily, and a very fine country.
Samuel Pepys, Diary (24 March 1669)

*The title page for Abraham Walter's book of maps of the Twisden Estate*

ON A STILL night in East Malling you can just hear a faint hum, swelling, fading, at times not discernible at all. It is generated a mile and a half to the north by the fast traffic twenty-four hours a day. The motorway was built in the late 1950s and it knocked another half-hour off the journey between London and the Continent. Traffic no longer had to struggle along the old turnpike through Maidstone to Hythe and Folkestone, though the turnpike itself had been the eighteenth century's hostage to progress: it cut the stage journey from Maidstone to London to a mere day. The coach left the Haunch of Venison or the Star in Maidstone High Street and four miles out of town, at Larkfield in the parish of East Malling, it stopped, then stopped again at the Swan in West Malling; and back to the turnpike.

The new motorway, the M 20, is a fine road. It is good to drive on and it cuts along the Malling valley, small in scale and ripe for wrecking by planners, but uplifting to the spirit. It is bounded on the north by the chalk downs, pierced north and south by the Medway, bounded on the south by the greensand ridge above the Medway's upstream curve towards Tonbridge, and beyond that, by the Weald, where careful husbandry raises hops, apples, cherries, and even grape vines and peaches and clementines, but which once was mile upon mile of unrelenting trees and marshes. On the greensand hills the M 20 is fast and firm, founded on ragstone and flint, the indigenous materials used by the conquering Normans on all their Kentish churches and halls, when the project wasn't magnificent enough to justify importing stone blocks from Caen. So the juggernaut transporters sweep into England, day and night, and the holiday-makers sweep out through the contractor-built motorway ravine that neatly splits the north of the parish — New Hythe, Gig Hill, Lunsford — from the rest of East Malling and Larkfield.

If you look from one of the high points in East Malling, from Well Street with Broadwater Farm at your back, the geography of most of the parish and a good deal of the valley can be dimly discerned: to the west the spire of the parish church of West Malling, blasted once by lightning but replaced in 1837 and soaring above its octave of bells. Further across in a clump of trees the massive tower built by Gundulf, the architect and bishop of Rochester Cathedral, for the eleventh-century Benedictine Abbey of Malling now restored to Anglican nuns of that order.

West Malling is the johnny-come-lately of the two Mallings. A century after Egbert granted a church to East Malling, his successor Edmund the Magnificent, king of the English from 940 to 946 and scourge of the Norsemen, granted land to 'my beloved' Bishop Buhric of Rochester:

'From the south bounds of the king's wood and from the king's wood to the boundary of the ville of Offham, and then to the military road and along that road over the Lillieburn to the boundary of East Malling. And from there southward from the east of the cross to the broad way towards the south in a direct line along the said way to the king's wood . . .' Allowing that the king's wood has been chopped down to make way for the West Malling Battle of Britain fighter station and that the military road is the A 20, then that grant of land to Rochester describes with some precision the boundaries of West Malling today.

West Malling was Malling Parva, Little Malling. But Gundulf's Abbey brought with it markets and fairs and tanners and brewers. The village grew and acquired the grace name Town Malling by which it is still often known; the manor of East Malling became part of the Abbey's possessions and took its turn as Parvas Meallingas.

North of the Mallings is the little tiled church of Leybourne with its gabled shrine in the chancel, said to contain the heart of Sir Roger de Leybourne, who died crusading in Palestine in 1271. Beyond that again is Snodland with its church by the ferry-point on the river where pilgrims to Canterbury once crossed, a village where a light powdering from the Blue Circle cement works covers everything greyly. To the east of East Malling, the modest tower of the little aisle-less Norman church of Ditton. Beyond that in Aylesford the massive oil burners of Reed's mills rear their bulk as a landmark from the Downs for ten miles around: Aylesford folk objected to their erection and were fobbed off with a derisory screen of trees.

Looking still from Well Street, in the foreground is Cobbs Hall Farm, the only real pastureland in East Malling, with its little herd of Jerseys. Beyond that, John Larking's Clare House set in its shrunken park before the mill pond. The county council built houses and two schools in the remainder of the park, with their own pub and shopping centre, so that though this is by far the most populous part of East Malling, it is separated from the centre of the village by the green band of what remains of the park.

Down in the hollow among the beeches and horse chestnuts is Mill Street, as old as Domesday: the high old Weir Mill with its white weatherboard turret and steep grey slate roof, the plumes of steam from Middle Mill, now a factory for making bubbly perry drinks with names like Wicked Lady, Calypso and Snowball, where the twenty-foot cylindrical vats stand sentinel with the mountainous stacked crates. Across the old horse pond and through the trees, the church, Court Lodge, the cluster of cottages in Church Walk, and the modern spec-built crescent of houses called The Grange, where the old vicarage was and long before that the Roman villa. And half a mile to the north of the church, Bradbourne, one of the finest Queen Anne houses in all England. Mill Street, High Street, Church Walk, Well Street, Bradbourne Park are in essence just as they were when Abraham Walter of Larkfield surveyed and mapped those parts of the parish that belonged to the lord of the manor, Sir Roger Twisden, second baronet, during the 1680s.

In Well Street are two timber-framed cottages which Sir Roger's father, Judge Thomas Twisden, bought when first he set his sights on East Malling during the Commonwealth. And outside the front door of one of them, Wellhead House, rises the spring that turns swiftly into the broad stream central to East Malling's fortunes over the centuries. Abraham Walter marked it '(St.)' on one of his maps and explained in a ponderous footnote: 'Where (St.) is there is the Springhead where ariseth that Stream, which Runneth downe by Bradborn, and through Ditton into the River Medway. S/ is the Stream as it Runneth from the Springhead &c.' A name would have helped, but neither before nor since has it had one, so it will be simplest to call it the mill stream.

Voles and weasels have their nests here, and moorhens and mallard ducks. The stream rises from five or six points and broadens immediately to twenty feet across, then flows through beds of cress then steep grassy banks between orchards under the railway and through the mill pond and over the mill race of the old Upper Mill. The rusting ratchet of the mill wheel is there, embedded in rock; so, too, the tall building where the rags were separated before being pulped for paper — degrading, filthy work: one of the scientists at East Malling Fruit Research Station remembers as a youngster hearing a neighbour painfully and interminably coughing up dust after shiftwork at the mill. Within a hundred yards the stream flows past the old Weir Mill, under Mill Street, through Middle Mill, then Lower Mill's pond in Clare Park, before it twists and turns, mostly underground since the advent of the housing estate, and emerges into Bradbourne Park. Here once it formed the moat around Tudor Bradbourne, but the third baronet rebuilt the house and dammed the stream to divert it and to form a lovely sickle-shaped lake before the southern door. Out of the park it flows, through the old Ditton corn mill, under the A20, and through what used to be Cobdown Farm before it became Reed paper mill playing fields. The rest is ignominious. The last mill has been crushed into the footings for the motorway and the stream itself now burrows underground and re-emerges stealthily through a concrete culvert into the Medway.

It isn't too fanciful to see in the map of the parish, with its broad southern boundary tapering irregularly to the north, the outlines of the map of England, and a walk from New Hythe — the parish port for centuries, now busier than ever but restricted to loading and unloading pulp and paper for the gigantic Reed paper mills — to the ragstone ridge is a walk through history, industrial, agricultural, and political. National events touched closely upon the Malling valley and upon the parish of East Malling and Larkfield, and local events mirrored the nation's.

The Romans built a big, elaborately decorated villa here, north of where the church now stands (the medieval church-builders used tiles from the Roman villa between courses of ragstone in the south chancel wall). The Britons or invading Norsemen burnt down the villa, probably in the fourth century. The Romans built a 'military road' east to west through the parish (their predecessors had used the track that stretches across the face of the North Downs between Winchester and Canterbury: now it is known as the Pilgrim's Way, but once it must have been used by traders and herdsmen from Cornwall and all points east). This road (now the A20) would have been used by Alfred when he marched to beat the Danes at Aylesford in 895, and by Edmund Ironsides when he repeated the operation in 1016. Egbert, the first king of England in all but name, founded a church in East Malling in about 827, perhaps to cement relations with his Archbishop of Canterbury and to celebrate his gift of the kingdom of Kent to his son Aethelwulf. At any rate, there remains the charter announcing his foundation, 'Hic dedit ecclesiae Christi villam quae Meallinges vocatur.' Archbishop Anselm presented the church of East Malling to the Abbey of West Malling, and Henry VIII returned it to Cranmer.

The lords of the manor grew rich on the tithes that came their way at the dissolution of the Abbey, but the poor of the parish starved and many emigrated to North America after the unsuccessful agricultural labourers' revolution of 1830 to escape the degradation of life on relief. The Court Baron met in Court Lodge beside the church, under the jurisdiction of the lord of the manor's steward and a jury of twelve good men and true, though not necessarily literate, and meted out justice and settled disputes about boundaries and footpaths. And as the power of the lord declined, John Larking arrived, a banker and timber merchant, one of the thrusting new breed of entrepreneur. He bought the mills in the parish and waxed rich. He caused the notable London architect Michael Searles to build him the domed, neo-classical Clare House. He bought from the fading Twisdens, he enclosed common lands, and he used parishioners as a front for the acquisition of yet more land. And when the master plan was complete, lo, he was master of all he surveyed: a park henceforth to be known as Clare Park and lands and riches greater than those of the lord of the manor. And in the slump after the final defeat of Napoleon, the Maidstone Bank of which he was founder and partner collapsed in the great crash of non-joint-stock country banks, and John Larking fled to live in Boulogne, a pattern of capitalist success and failure that has been followed to this day.

The mills that Larking once commanded spread now across the boundary into Aylesford, over fields and water meadows. Reels of paper are manufactured in huge sheds and dispatched to the machine room in Fleet Street of the *Daily Mirror*, sufficient for a sale of four million copies a day. The stream that rises at Springhead in East Malling still supplies water for this newsprint, but no longer all: now the resources of the Medway are needed as well.

For Kent is not just the garden of England; it has always been an industrial county as well. The Romans made bricks and tiles here in great quantities, and brick and tile is still the distinguishing mark of the county's building. A seam of brick earth runs through East Malling (and there's another seam of fulling earth which, when wool was king, not paper, was trodden into rough cloth in the mills and then washed out taking the grease with it). The iron industry started in the forests of the Weald. The Romans used this iron, and the wood of the forest for smelting it. England's navy was furnished with guns founded in the Weald and down in the old iron villages of Kent there are even iron gravestones from the time of that industrial prosperity. There are coal mines in East Kent, shipyards and naval docks in North Kent, and between Rochester and East Malling on the west bank of the Medway, the cement works of Halling and Snodland.

In the fifteen miles the motorway stretches between Wrotham and Leeds Castle, where eight of England's medieval queens lived, the motorists flash by four thousand years of history. For two miles north-east of East Malling crossroads is the first manageable ford upstream on the Medway. Here is a fourteenth-century bridge, the gabled high street of Aylesford, and the church high above trees and river among the beeches: Kent's most clichéd view, repeated in engravings, on calendars, on book jackets: an artificial flower planted in blood. Here came the neolithic invaders from the Continent, their necropolis all over the slopes of the Medway marked by the Countless Stones, by the remains of nameless barrows and cromlechs, by Kits Coty House, which isn't a house at all but three vertical seven-foot sarsen stones with a horizontal capstone thirteen feet long on top: tidily fenced in and disappointing to blasé modern man, but to the indefatigable Samuel Pepys, who passed by in the last year of his diary, an object of wonder: 'Had the pleasure of seeing the Medway running, winding up and down mightily,' he noted first, and then reported of the matter at hand: 'Not so big as those on Salsbury-plain, but certainly it is a thing of great antiquity.'

But most importantly for East Malling — and for England — the warriors Hengist and Horsa came to Aylesford, defeated Vortigern, and drove the Celts out of Kent. So legend has it, at any rate, and a pile of flints called the Horsted is romantically said to mark Horsa's burial place at Aylesford. However that may be, one of the Jutish tribes involved in the fighting settled on the ragstone loam above the river, the fertile strip between the chalk downs and the forested and marsh-ridden Weald.

Lambarde, the sixteenth-century antiquary from Sevenoaks who wrote one of the earliest of travel books, *Perambulations in Kent*, took a stab at the origin of the place-name of East Malling, which he had found in the Cartularium Saxonium of 942–6 as East Meallinga (Meallingis, Meal-ingan, Mallinges, Estmallinges, Estmalling, Estmauling, Mauling, Meaulling, Est Meaulling are other variants for East and West Malling in medieval documents; and in Domesday Book East Malling appears as Metlinges and West Malling as Mellingetes). 'Malling,' Lambarde wrote, 'in Saxon, Mealing . . . that is, the Low place flourishing with meal, or Corne, for so it is everywhere accompted.' Furthermore, he added, 'A man (but meanly exercised in their language) may (for the most part) as readily understand the Scite, or soile, of their townes, by the onely sound of the name, as by the verie sight of the place it selfe.' The modern work, *The Place-Names of Kent*, by Judith Glover, flatly contradicts Lambarde: 'Malling, East and West (pronounced Mawlin). Mealla's people . . . East Malling seems to have been the original settlement of this tribe. . . .' And the great authority on Kentish place-names, J. K. Wallenberg, comes to no conclusion at all after a very long argument.

The village itself, the bit people mean when they say East Malling, the bit with the church and the red-brick and white-sash Queen Anne Court Lodge, and the King and Queen pub (the king and queen were William and Mary), and the antique shop in a Tudor Wealden cottage that was built before Newcastle coal came by sailing barge up the Thames to London and up the Medway to the parish of New Hythe, so that it had a recessed, high central hall and a hearth in the middle of the floor and a hole in the roof to let the smoke out — this bit of the village huddles still by the crossroads formed by the junction of Church Walk, High Street, New Road, which was new in 1676, and Mill Street, where Domesday recorded two of the new-fangled water mills: important, since there were only 140 mills distributed among 347 settlements at the time.

So on the face of it there has been little enough change. Yet when Daniel Hill, the vicar in 1776, reported back to the Archbishop of Canterbury with his unofficial census figures (to which he added the proud rider: 'I have no Dissenters in this Parish, nor have I on Enquiry found that there has been above one for many years past' — though soon there was to be a Wesleyan chapel, now vanished), he assessed a population of 953 in 175 houses; the 1971 national census figures show East Malling with a population of 10,955 in 3,245 households. This is because out of sight of the crossroads the parish's population explosion has happened on big estates straddling the A20.

For the Domesday mills were caught up in the industrial revolution. The original two grew to four within as many hundred yards: Upper Mill, where they manufactured the paper for the rupee notes that financed the jewel in England's crown — the mill today, like the Raj, is a ruin; Weir Mill, now a furniture warehouse, its brick and board falling into gentle dilapidation; Middle Mill, once at the fore in developing writing papers for the new middle classes; and Lower Mill, vanished altogether though its mill pond remains as a small ornamental swan lake in Clare Park.

Here the paper industry of Britain had part of its beginning. But the industry outgrew these mills and moved to the north of the parish. For the small village clustered around the church of St James is only part of the story. The river Medway flows from Tonbridge eastwards through the Wealden orchards and hop gardens, describes a huge U-turn through Maidstone and then flows back eastwards through Allington and Aylesford and New Hythe and Snodland, where it turns again and flows out northwards through a gap in the chalk downs to Rochester and Chatham. North and south, the parish is roughly circumscribed by the Medway's U-turn. From the northern boundary of the parish on the Medway to the southern boundary high on the ragstone ridge above the southern loop of the Medway at Wateringbury (George Orwell's terminus when he went slumming it with the hop pickers) is a walk of four miles, and between the eastern and western boundaries east of Eden Farm and west of the field called Ditton Rough is a little under two miles.

The stream, the roads, the river have been the village's fortune. And the village's fortune until the Reformation meant the fortune of the Abbey, and afterwards, of the lords of the manor, the Twisdens. Henry VIII's rule marked the beginnings of a great age for the gentry. The Reformation had released untold wealth. A few of the gentry chose still to glorify God and spend money on sacred ends: Hugh Catlyn, who lived at Bradbourne during the troublesome reigns of Henry VIII and his papist daughter Mary, completed the transition of St James's to Perpendicular Gothic in the late 1540s *after* the Reformation. But by and large this was the great age of secular spending, and after the uncertainty of the Civil War and the Commonwealth, the farming gentry became rich beyond the dreams of avarice. Everywhere, the new classicism, which came into England in the designs of Inigo Jones in the time of the first two Stuarts, began to catch on. Mr Wren, later Sir Christopher, was all the rage. Damp old Tudor granges were definitely not *à la mode*. Passing through Kent on horseback at about this time, the intrepid Celia Fiennes remarked of the medieval Penshurst Place, 'the house is but old'. She was scarcely more dismissive of Hadrian's Wall.

In the parish to the south of East Malling, the Style family had already built Wateringbury Place in the fashionable mode of Queen Anne's reign, red brick and white sash, with lawns and waterfalls and a little lake. Soon and more grandly Horace Walpole's friend Robert Mann was to build Linton Place five miles away with, as Walpole wrote, 'the whole county its garden'. And Walpole was even more enchanted by the Palladian splendour of the Earl of Westmorland's Mereworth Castle over the hill, which cost £100,000 and, Walpole wrote, 'is so perfect in a Palladian taste that I must own it has recovered me a little from Gothic'. Lord Westmorland earned the praise. After all, had he not razed an entire village of his tenants to provide a fit setting for his new home? Not to mention their old church. (With the replacement for this, at least, Walpole had some fun: the steeple, he observed, 'seems designed for the latitude of Cheapside, and is so tall that the poor church curtsies under it, like Mary Rich in a vast high-crown hat.')

Sir Thomas Twisden, the third baronet of Bradbourne, was more modest than his neighbour. He retained the Tudor cellars, the roof of the great hall, and most of the Tudor ground plan, and he caused his house to be rebuilt around the old foundations. It is an informal but rhythmic design with a portico and rectangular and oval windows interspersed with blind arches across the façades of varicoloured brick, elegantly rubbed and turned in imitation of classical motifs. Twisden owned brick-fields on East Malling Heath: within the parish or without, there was no need for Sir Thomas to turn far to find brickmakers or skilled bricklayers.

To be a Twisden was to be a power in the land. Judge Twisden was able to give sanctuary for the rest of his life to the Cromwellian colonel-of-horse who escorted Charles I to the scaffold; the man was called Mathew Thomlinson, and he just happened to be the judge's brother-in-law (they are both buried in the church). He was able to send Bunyan back to prison and to gaol the father of the Quakers, George Fox.

When a new kind of power took over the land in the nineteenth century — the power of industry, the rampant power of investment capital — even then, when the Twisdens were in decline, ravaged by a family dispute, with no male heir apparent, the women members of the family went out into the village and dispensed flannel petticoats and jackets to the poor, and on 23 December received six well-behaved children at Bradbourne and gave them shirts and frocks and cake and apples and nuts with a glass of wine each: a Dickensian coda to the patronage that this house had once deployed.

For the poor were always with them, but the degree of poverty among the poor varied through the centuries. The standard of living in rural England at any given time is a matter for argument: economic historians still cannot decide whether agricultural labourers were worse off in 1830 at the time of the rick-burnings and machine-breakings than they had been in 1760. Merrie Englande had never been that merrie. But when William Cobbett looked back in anger, he was looking from the vantage-point of a man who had been born a peasant but had seen in his own life-time the whole class of peasantry converted into the world's first agricultural proletariat, from being part of the farmer's household to being hired hands without even the freedom to move from parish to parish to seek work.

National averages do not help the argument in a period when prosperity varied so much from region to region:

A gentleman of Wales
A knight of Cales
A Lord of the North Country,
A yeoman of Kent
With one year's rent
Could buy them out all three.

The rhyme had enough currency for there to be some truth in it, just as there was some truth in the proud assertion that Kent never had villein labour: the *villani* of Domesday were copyhold tenants. By 1830 the Kentish agricultural labourer was in the same groove of poverty as all others, thrown back on to parish relief to keep body and soul, wife and family together even when he was in work. But when Judge Twisden was lord of the manor, the contrast between his wealth and the possessions of the meanest labourer was wide, but not demeaning.

In his will made in 1675, Sir Thomas left his estate to his son and heir Roger and his lands to his widow Jane to revert to Roger upon her death. To his daughter Elinor who was about to marry and to his daughter Jane who was already married, he left £1,000 each. To his daughters Margaret and Elizabeth he left £2,000 each if they married with their mother's consent, or upon her death. To his sons Thomas, William, Heneage, and Francis, he gave £1,000 each.

> Also I doo give unto my loving wife £500 and all such coynes of gold and silver as are kept by her. . . . Also I doe give unto every of my Sonnes and Daughters and to my Daughter in Law the wife of my Sonne Roger Twisden and to the Wifes of my Son Thomas and William Twisden, and to my Nephew Sir William Twisden, to each of them 20 shillings to buy them a Ring in remembrance of mee. And I do further give unto the poor of East Malling £10 to be distributed by my executrix to such as shee shall thinke fitt. Then I give unto my servant Thomas Brandon and to my servant William Hoole £10 apeece if they be liveing with mee at the tyme of my death. And to every other of my servants that shall be liveing with me at the time of my death, twenty shillings apeece. And to every of the servants that shall be servants unto my son Roger Twisden at the tyme of my death 10s apiece. And I further give unto my old servant Roger Mills for the better enabling to putt his sonne Thomas Mills my Godsonne to bee an Apprentice £10 if I doo not pay to him in my life tyme.

That was on the grand scale, but the lot of the meanest of villagers was far from pitiable. Matthew Wyborne, a labourer, died in 1692 bequeathing 'to my loving wife Dorothy Wyborne all that one messuage or tenement one kitchen one Barne, one Stable one outhouse one garden and two orchard with their outhouses in Millstreete in East Malling', to pass to his son, James Wyborne, also a labourer, upon his wife's death. And this is by no means an unusual will.

By the nineteenth century many yeomen, unless they were in trade, would be unlikely to leave those sorts of possessions. Labourers were even worse off. Family names that had appeared in village records over the centuries as jurymen and witnesses in the lord's Court Baron and to the beating of bounds and even as the founders of charities turned up now on the records of parish relief, names like Furner and Allchin.

And the true story of the parish poor is buried in the overseers' account books, a litany of parish relief sought and doled out, or not. It was a time when the vicar, with the small tithes awarded to him in the fourteenth century (the Abbey's great tithes went now, of course, to the Twisdens), was at odds with his flock, the poor and the employers of the poor, who resented the fruits of their labour going, unearned as they saw it, to the parson. For by the time the tithe commissioners reported in 1842, the vicar's tithes were worth £802 a year to the Revd S. F. Godmond. The sum for which the agricultural labourers had rioted a few years earlier and been hanged or deported was 2s.3d. a day in winter and 2s.6d. a day in summer.

The humbler in Mr Godmond's parish left no records of their affairs. On 3 November 1830 the labourers had a mass wage meeting in East Malling, but there is no mention of it in the minutes of the parish governing body, the vestry, which met two days later, though the vestry did resolve to chase up parishioners in arrears with poor rates. A few weeks later the vestry recorded: 'It were also ordered that the overseer write to Mr Stevenson to inform him, that he is directed to apply to the Bench of Magistrates to enforce the payment of £50 now due for poor rate from the Revd S. F. Godmond on the 31st Inst. unless the amount is paid on or before that time.' Three churchwardens headed the list of signatories.

The troubles spread from Kent through all the southern counties. What kept the countryside from revolution no one can say. Certainly Armageddon was expected. It shows in Cobbett's warnings in the *Political Register*, it shows in the speeches of the radical politician John Cartwright, the Father of Reform, it shows in the letters of Thomas Law Hodges, M.P. for West Kent, who had married Rebecca Twisden, daughter of the sixth baronet, and commuted between Parliament, Bradbourne, and his own family home in Cranbrook. Cartwright was his uncle, and they corresponded regularly. Through Cartwright, Hodges knew William Cobbett. In spite of the shared political interests of the three men, Hodges showed early signs of not wishing to be associated too closely with them in public affairs. He was ambitious for success and he nurtured the middle ground of politics. He was a man of property, and when trouble came close to home, he made it clear that he stood on the side of law and property against the labourers, though his Commons speeches were liberal (in so far as this book has a villain, Hodges, as will later be seen, is the man).

Yet Cobbett, the hater of injustice, the tribune of the people whose own speeches in Kent and Sussex were held by many to be the spark that set off the troubles, was clearly on very friendly terms with Hodges. On 3 October 1833, when his life's work, reform, had succeeded in Parliament but in a grievously watered-down form, here is Cobbett, lively as ever, writing from Maidstone to Bradbourne:

Dear Sir,

You will naturally wonder how I can be here, and not avail myself of the opportunity of having the honour to wait on you. The case is this: it is a short question with me. *Beagles*, or *No cabbages*, of which I have a field that would have 30 tons to the one *next May*, and which will not have an ounce, if I do not kill the hares; and, I know that they cannot be killed without a parcel of Banham Beagles.

On an expedition to find these, I and my son William sallied out from the Wen on Monday, thinking to go no further than Croydon, having heard that there were some there. The information was false; but we got a faint scent which took us on to Addington (4 miles); the sort was, part terrier, nose too sharp, legs too long and slender; but, we were told that there was some *in Kent*! That was a large space indeed; but, on we came, urged by the peril of the Cabbages, to *Westerham*, having, at Limpsfield, got scent of Beagles at Crockham, near Westerham. Got a couple, and ordered them off to Bolt-Court. Then, hearing of some at Otford, and cheered by our late success, we pushed on Tuesday morning to Otford. The Miller gone to London!

Guess you at my expression heaped on the Wen for having seduced away the Miller. But, trying back, we found a dog and a bitch at the Bat-and-Ball in the parish of Riverhead. Made *sure* of these and (lying *so near*) went on to learn what success had attended Major Waythe, to whom I had written on the subject.

But, now, as *Tuesday night* approached, and we were approaching Maidstone, we recollected, that we were 40 miles from the printing-office, and that there was *no Register* written! The printer must have it on *Thursday* by post, or else! Under such circumstances, it was too hazardous to encounter the hop-gossip and political botheration of Maidstone. Turned off and went by Aylsford to the House on

Penenden Heath, where we might expect to be able to write for an 'entire' day, as the blarnying Irish would call it. Rose at six, set to work, I dictating and my son writing, closed at 8 o'clock, and sent off the lashing for Dr Black, by my son, at about 9 o'clock, he taking one of the dogs with him.

'Well,' you will say, 'but why not take *both*? And why could not you (having finished Dr Black) come over here, and see the bags of hops that are to fetch bags of gold?'

He could not take the *two*; for one of them (though we had *made sure* of her) had gnawed the string assunder, and had (as one suppose) gone back to 'the Bat and Ball'; and I cannot go to see the piles of hop bags, because I must go back (16 miles) to 'the Bat and Ball' for the bitch; and must be *in London tomorrow*.

Waythe tells me, that you have been so good as to promise to assist me in this my state of 'agricultural distress'. Perhaps you will be able to find time to give me a line on the subject, directed, always, to Bolt-Court, Fleet Street.

I hope that all your other several affairs have been as prosperous as that of the hops; and I always am,

Dear Sir

Your faithful

And most obedient servant

WM COBBETT

The letter is characteristic of English society. Tithes were the enemy, and taxes, and machinery; but there was no visible class enemy. Mereworth, with its village destroyed to make a vista, was an exception. In France, châteaux of that sort were the rule. In England the lords of the manor were farmers. The Duke of Dorset hired hands at Knole on the basis of their skills at cricket, and when Kent beat All-England in 1743 one of the Duke's sons was playing, but the captain of the side was Val Romney, one of the Duke's gardeners: officers and men to this day drop formalities when they play in the same sports team for the honour of the regiment. All chaps together. And when a group of farmers and labourers in 1830 planned to force a tax-collector to disgorge the booty he had collected so that farmers could pay decent wages, the labourers themselves decided to desist on the grounds that 'it was the king's money and it wouldn't do'.

The age of high farming in the middle of the century did more for the poor than village relief in the first place or the Poor Law of 1834 in the second; and cricket remained the means for dispelling aggression. In 1880 two hundred men of East Malling celebrating a cricket match at the Bull in Larkfield, by the entrance to Bradbourne, heard that in a cottage opposite was the police informer who had caused the arrest of the Bull's landlord on a charge of receiving stolen beer. They tore the cottage apart, literally, to exact revenge. The informer escaped by tunnelling through a wall into the cottage next door and thirteen of the rioters faced charges of criminal damage and assembling to 'disturb the peace of our Lady the Queen'.

The informer, Goodhew, bore an ancient name in East Malling, and so did some of the rioters. Almost none of those names exist in the parish today. The agricultural revolution and the industrial revolution have done their work. Machinery reduced the need for hands. Factories drew rural workers to the towns and cities. Railways and roads and cheap fuel for transport made commuting from twenty, thirty, fifty miles out of London a possibility, then an inevitability, and the countryside became a suburb for us, the commuters. The vast growth of capital-intensive industry meant that most people's working lives no longer took any account of the seasons. The old verities vanished. The countryside near London became green belt, protected like an historic monument, though more precariously.

We know all this, but does it matter? Is the history worth recording, and is it relevant to life today? Or is it, as the man said, bunk? The Medway gap is on the Government list for development, which is the planner's euphemism for bricks and mortar, regulation-width grass verges and high-fenced allotments so that kids don't wreck the crops because they have nothing better to do because there is nothing to do because you can't transplant communities the way you can cabbage seedlings. And Bradbourne, once the manor house, is now the headquarters of the Fruit Research Station. And the mills employ labour from Chatham and Rochester and Gillingham and Maidstone. And Larkfield Heath isn't heath but houses. And down by the Medway, Brook (which the commissioners drained and allotted as agricultural land in the village's Enclosure Act of 1810) is the site for bigger and bigger warehouses which will be visited by bigger and bigger juggernauts if the transport lobbies get their way, which they will. And Borough Court Farm no longer grows hops, but Kleenex tissues. And the last farm on the mill stream, Mill Hall, is a wreck bounded by a scrapyard.

But it is too early for elegies. Domesday recorded in 1085:

In the lath of Aylesford, in Larkfield hundred, the same archbishop [Canterbury] himself holds East Malling in demesne. It was taxed at two sulings. There is arable land for seven teams. In demesne there are three teams. And thirty-eight villeins with twelve bordars have five teams. There is a church. And five slaves. And two mills of ten shillings. And twenty-one acres of meadow. Wood of sixty hogs. In aggregate value in the time of King Edward it was worth nine pounds. Likewise, when he received it. And now, as much. And yet it renders fifteen pounds.

Even in English translation that leaves room for argument, not least about the land measurements. Domesday mentions a church. It mentions mills. It mentions agriculture and agricultural labourers. It mentions taxes. The pigs have gone; the rest are still with us. And the history of the village is not just in entries in ancient documents. It can be read in the land. When a builder rips out an old hedgerow, he might be obliterating nine hundred years of history. The soil is what it is because of at least two thousand years of cultivation. Land became property, agriculture became money-making industry, but the land in a wider sense still belongs to the people and is not lightly to be given up for other uses. History begins at home, and we need to understand these things, because without understanding the word of the expert and the bureaucrat becomes law: another motorway, another housing estate.

Meanwhile planning priorities change, fashion swings from building new estates, new towns, to renovating the interiors of the decaying cities and giving them new life. Larkfield is urban, scarred beyond redemption by petrol stations and warehouses. But when a planner in County Hall in Maidstone decided that the area needed a shopping centre with super-markets and car parks and electricity showrooms in the neighbouring parish of Leybourne, the villagers stood up and resisted. Perhaps grass-roots democracy — and never was the cliché more apt — can speak out at last on this close matter of the way we are to live.

# 2 God's 2-and-a-bit per cent

**... one does feel that one is in a respectable profession, as it were.** The Revd. Richard Lea

*Court Lodge Farm in 1684 from Walter's maps of the Twisden Estate*

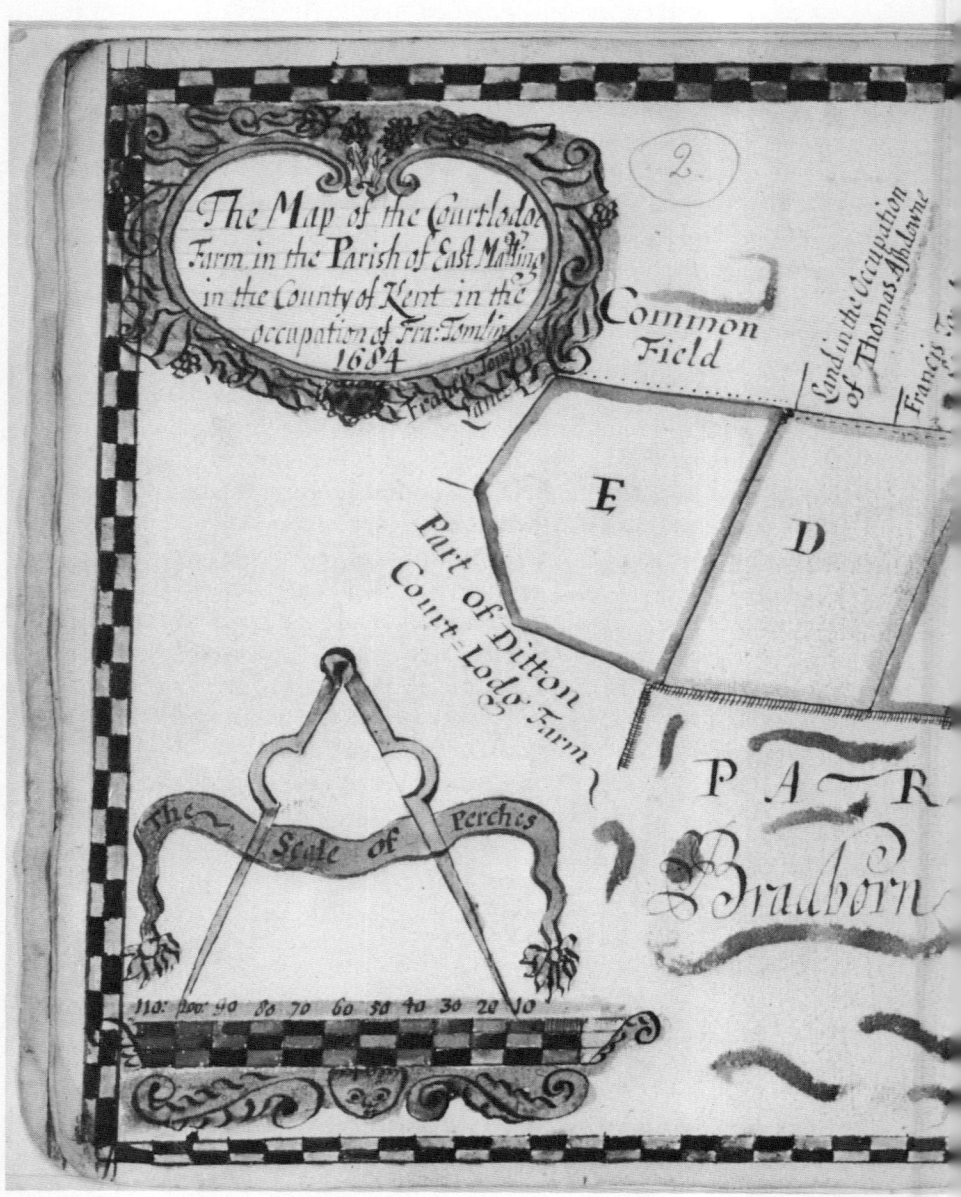

IN 1956 THE vicar of St James's spotted a crack running down through the stone fabric of the tower. It was clear that the bells would have to stop ringing, for the second time since 1695. In any case the bells themselves needed a new timber frame, so sooner or later they would have to be taken down and rehung. The vicar wrote to the Whitechapel Bell Foundry and asked them to examine the belfry and make a quotation for

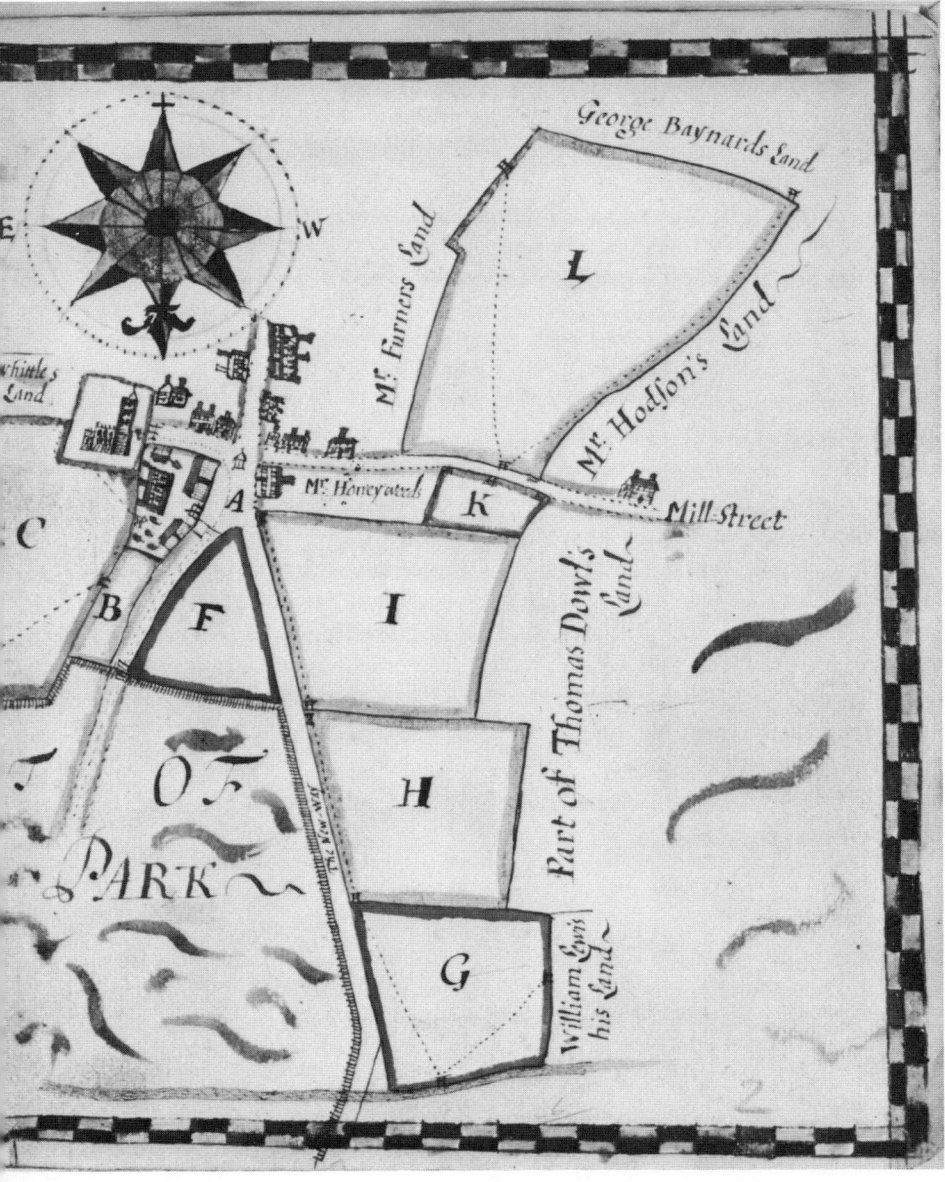

the work. The master founder wrote back: Dear Sir, Thank you for your letter. We have not heard from you since 1885. . . .

Whitechapel Bell Foundry was the natural firm to undertake the work: they had cast and hung the original great tenor bell and its four companions in 1695, they added the treble bell in 1831, and they rehung all the bells in 1885. For nearly three hundred years the bells cast by James Bartlet (each embossed *James Bartlet me fecit*) have pealed for the weddings, funerals, and church services of East Malling folk.

For the church's heartbeat is measured not in weeks or in months or in years, but in generations. And the church is the heart of the parish, a surprisingly long building for Kent with, unusually for a parish church, the clerestory lights carried right through above. Hugh Catlyn of Bradbourne built the battlements on the tower the length of the building. A pious man and a plain one: he left the inscription *Hugh Catlyn built this*. His successors, five Misses Twisden who lived at Bradbourne right through the second half of the nineteenth century, had the battlements repaired after a fire and Charlotte Twisden noted anxiously in her diary: 'Lane's bill for the chancel came in. The whole sum amounts to £388.1.3½. We got for the old lead £59.11.5 which leaves it £328.9.10½. It was quite £100 more than we expected but we shall no doubt soon be able to pay it up.'

But the battlements are simply part of the stylish sixteenth-century face-lift. A mile to the north-east the little St Peter-ad-Vincula in Ditton shows how St James's — or rather St Mary's, as the East Malling church was called until well after the Marian festivals were abolished at the Reformation (there's a small modern statue in remembrance of Our Lady in a niche above a pier in the nave) — must have looked in Norman times. Under successive abbesses the building grew: it gained a chancel, north and south aisles and a south porch, clerestory lights, a taller tower: Early English, Decorated, Perpendicular. Then, two hundred years ago, the parishioners commissioned a clock from the blacksmith which, blue and gold, runs still; but on electricity.

So the tower — up to the string course above the clock anyway — has looked down towards the mills for a thousand years. Longer, that is, than the list of vicars reaches back, though that stumbles more or less uneventfully to the twentieth century from William de Wrotham in 1206, filled with names known only because they filled the incumbency for a period, but with occasional exceptions. There was Richard Adams, well-respected enough to merit a brass in the floor of the chancel when he died in 1522. Thirty-four years later John Wells was installed, 'presented by the serene princes Philip and Mary, King and Queen of England', as Cardinal Pole, the Primate, recorded more in papist fervour than strict fact, since Philip of Spain never succeeded in extending his dominion to these shores. But most notable of all was the vicar of 1363, Sir John Lorkyn, who protested in anger at the Abbey's tax on his living and received the grant from Simon, Archbishop of Canterbury, of

> the mansion belonging to the vicarage, with the garden of it, and six acres and three roods of arable land, and two acres of meadow, which they used to have in past times, free and discharged from the payment of tithes, together with the herbage of the cemetery of the church, and the trees growing on it, and the tithes of silva cedua, lambs, wool, pigs, geese, ducks, eggs, chicken, calves, cheese, and the produce of the dairy, pidgeons, hemp, and flax, apples, pears, pasture, honey, wax beans planted in gardens, and of all other seeds whatsoever sown in them, and also the tithes of sheaves arising from orchards or gardens, dug with the foot, together with the tithes as well of the cattle of the religious in their manors and lands wheresoever situated within the parish, either bred up, feeding, or lying there, and of all other matters above mentioned, being within the said manors and lands, as of the cattle and matters of this sort of all others whatsoever, arising within the parish. . . .

Today the vicar is Derek Chapman. Though well into his fifties he is a local cricketer of renown, but definitely not a muscular Christian. He does not make converts in the King and Queen public house, though he does enjoy a scotch and soda at home when he has guests. His wife Daphne drinks sherry. He is not a hands-across-the-ecumenical-gap man and he doesn't rise to the bait when Daphne mildly joshes him about it.

Like many vicars who cannot afford the things their parishioners can — holidays abroad, colour television — he sends his son to be privately educated just as he was himself. There are those among his flock who feel his relationship with them is a bit padre-and-other-ranks. As a matter of fact, Derek Chapman was a career army officer, but not a padre. He left the army in 1952 to study at Cambridge University for the Church. He says it was his wife who convinced him that he had a vocation. She strenuously denies this, but it is obviously a standing joke between them. Her family always blame her, she says, for having persuaded Derek to give up a safe job in the army to be as poor as a church mouse. There is no doubt that they found it tough financially at first; it remains difficult. Unlike most of the women in the congregation, this vicar's wife works for a living, in a laboratory at 'the Research', as the Fruit Research Station is known locally: she has a science degree. And she has started taking piano examinations (she is up to grade 8) so that when she retires she can supplement their pittance by giving music lessons to children.

A few of the congregation come from the oldest housing estate, Clare Park (a lot of villagers settled there: the later estates are populated by people from Maidstone and London). The rest of the congregation live in the old village. Most of those who are not retired (and there is quite a high proportion of young churchgoers) work as teachers, lawyers, farmers, civil servants, and a good sprinkling are scientists from the Research. The women's liberation movement has not caught up with the wives, perhaps because they don't need it. They bring up families, run the housewives' group and the W.I. They sing in the choir and the mildly secular offshoot called East Malling Singers. They used to train at the home of their choirmistress, Belinda Hunter (whose husband is at the Research), but there are three dozen or so of them now so they use the church instead, and in winter they turn up with blankets, hot-water bottles, scarves, sweaters; anything to keep warm while they sing. Some of these good people vote Liberal in the elections, but most feel more comfortably at home with the Conservatives. St James's stands behind a great yew at the end of Church Walk, a road flanked by a small Wealden hall-house (now an antique shop), some nineteenth-century cottages, and the Court Lodge, where the abbesses held the manor court, as did the Twisdens after they had rebuilt it at the same period as Bradbourne. Inside the church, the Twisdens blocked up the north and south windows of the chancel to erect marble testaments to the eternal memory of the family, and the bones of those who swore fealty to them in the manor court fill the churchyard: the Tomlins, the Whittles, the Furners and the Turners, the Maylems, the Blundens, the Goldings, the Thornhills and the Pottses, and the Allchins — yeomen, mostly, though a twentieth-century Allchin whose remains repose here reached the eminence of surgeon extraordinary to King George V.

By the west door a stone slab commemorates Mary Baker, a widow, for her remarkable feat of living until 1753, when she was a hundred and five. And in the east wall is a memorial to Sir Roger Twisden's exemplary servant, who died in 1751 aged forty-seven: 'as he lived beloved so he Dyed Lamented.'

The contrast of St James's with the other parish church, a mile north, could hardly be greater. Holy Trinity, Larkfield, stands dramatically on a hill a hundred yards from the chasm of the motorway that neatly bisects Larkfield. But even from the Medway at New Hythe its flamboyant Gothic is clearly not the real thing. It has been there only since 1854.

It wasn't the first house of God in the north of the parish. There had been 'the Chapell within the parishe of Est Mallynge called Newe Hithe', of which 'the First Fowder or donoure of the said Chappell and medowe ys not knowen, but there hath allwayes beene masse Celebrated within the same'. It in fact was the chantry chapel of St John; and following the indefatigable initiative of Henry VIII — for whom, as one of his biographers wrote, financial necessity was once more the mother of theological invention — Edward VI abolished the chantry in 1548 and sold the land.

Three hundred years later, Larkfield and New Hythe were hardly bigger than in Tudor times, but the Wigan family had moved to the parish. They were successful bankers who had taken over Clare House from the failed banker John Larking and the patronage of St James's from the fading Twisdens. They put their own sons into St James's as vicars, and they caused Holy Trinity to be built, as a chapel of ease to St James's; conveniently enough, the Wigans were able to install relatives as curates.

Close to, and even more so inside, Holy Trinity's Early English detail is endearing. The church is approached up a flight of steps through an elaborate lych-gate. There is a quirky open bell gable with three small bells; the whole edifice is massively buttressed; there are grouped lancet windows, two in the west wall below a big wheel window, three in the east; gargoyles; a tiled south porch leading into the only aisle; four-bay nave; small chancel; chancel arch rising on each side from luxuriant stone foliage; stone font with angels and angel corbels supporting roof beams, great crown posts at the centre. Blue and red glass in the lancets, blue and mauve in the wheel. Propped against the walls of the chancel, paintings by Sunday School infants announcing *Jesus Is Here*; piles of New English Bibles stacked in the pews; a bookcase neatly filled with hymnbooks by the door.

Holy Trinity was ready the year after Ruskin's second volume of *The Stones of Venice* pronounced: 'Now, all Gothic may be divided into two vast schools, one early, the other late; of which the former [is] noble, inventive, and progressive . . . the latter, ignoble, uninventive, and

declining. . . .' Ruskin would not have approved the melodrama of Larkfield; he might have noted the loving care.

For the curate the Wigans built a house in the same ragstone as the
church, but after Larkfield became an ecclesiastical parish in its own
right in 1949 the diocese sold that and acquired for the vicar a non-
descript detached brick house with a garage and a panel of imitation
weatherboarding above the front door; a house like any one from a
thousand housing estates. Once the vicar could see over the sloping
meadows to the river, but one of the proliferating paper firms built a
prefabricated warehouse in the meadow below the house and blocked the
view. St James's vicarage on the other hand is a handsome house standing back from the High Street, early nineteenth-century white stucco
façade concealing a much older, slightly sprawling brick building with a
big lawn and a kitchen garden and the stream that rises at Gillets Hole
flowing through and forming a rock pool big enough to bathe in.

The Revd Richard Lea, the vicar at Larkfield, is too unworldly and
too dedicated to work to rue the lost view or mourn the old Larkfield.
Hardly anything of the old hamlet survives apart from the row of cottages where the London road toll used to be, and the Bull Inn. Larkfield
House has gone and Larkfield Heath. There is a Methodist chapel in
coffee-bar-pagoda style instead of the smithy on the corner of New Hythe
Lane, a shopping centre round a neat square, a vegetable garden where
gallows once stood, a warning and a retribution, and streets and streets
of houses with well-kept lawns and flowers.

Mr Lea is a young, intelligent, energetic, and popular priest serving in
his first incumbency. Like Derek Chapman, he studied theology at Cambridge: he took his degree at the University, felt he had a calling, and
worked at theology at Westcote House for another two years. Sense of
vocation apart, he likes the Church because it is, he says, full of able men:
not necessarily at local level, but within the career structure: 'So one
does feel that one is in a respectable profession, as it were, from that point
of view, whether one is ambitious or not.'

Before Larkfield, he was a curate at Edenbridge, on the river Eden near
the Kent border with Surrey. Paradise could not be lost soon enough for
Richard Lea; as a curate he was underemployed; as a social man he
could not afford to reciprocate when people asked him and his wife to
dine. Larkfield did not bring untold wealth either, though he isn't
grumbling. He runs a small car and a small family. 'I was just looking at
my pay the other day. It's not far short of three and a half thousand now,
plus a house. Well, that's not bad. There are travelling expenses. And I

pay less in tax than I receive in family benefits. So I mean in Larkfield it's O.K. I wouldn't feel the same I think if I were still in a stockbrokerish parish like Edenbridge.'

He had been warned that Larkfield was a dreadful parish, all new estates with a floating population, young professionals without roots. But the warnings went in one ear and out the other. In Larkfield the private housing heavily outnumbers council housing: out of 2,000 houses only between 300 and 400 are council houses. These 2,000 houses represent an adult population of around 4,000, rising all the time because a big new estate is being built. And out of this 4,000 Richard Lea has a congregation of between 120 and 130. That is not the number of people you would find in church each Sunday, but an aggregate of the normal attendance at service, the number on the electoral roll, and the number which goes on high days and holidays.

Richard Lea slides open a card-index cabinet. 'Here's a sample of what people do for a living: this man's an insurance agent, monumental mason, a sales rep — lots of those — sales adviser, computer operator, engineering draughtsman, electrical designer, compositor, a flooring contractor, a panel beater, a fitter and turner, a driver, a machine man (that'll be at Reeds), bus mechanic, telecommunications, paper maker, bank officer, carpenter and joiner, lithographer, printer's order clerk (hmm, a lot in the printing trade), P.O. engineer, and again, mill worker, labourer, printer (yes!), truck repairer, warehouse supervisor. It's all within the same sort of range, though, isn't it. Buyer, surveyor, fireman — I've come across a lot of firemen, not necessarily working locally — a section leader — that'll be at Reeds I expect — vehicle removal officer: I remember that bloke, he works up in London and his job is to tow away parked cars and pound them for the police. Printing assistant — surprising number in the printing trade — an inspector, don't know what kind of inspector, graphic designer, chartered accountant — that's unusual — computer operator, civil servant, representative, trimmer, boiler operator. The other day I had the daughter of a kiln burner marry the son of a roll grinder.'

So Larkfield is everything Richard Lea had been warned, a transient population, few native to the area, only 2-and-a-bit per cent even occasional churchgoers. At the neighbouring parish of Leybourne, where there is only a curate and Richard Lea is priest-in-charge, 12 per cent of the population are churchgoers. At Larkfield the vicar has been on the church council longer than anyone except one of the church wardens. At Leybourne there are half a dozen parochial church councillors who have served since before Richard Lea was born. So at Larkfield they're game for anything. It's the sort of place, Mr Lea feels irreverently, where if something is advertised one evening on television, the next day it's sold out in Larkfield.

But contrary to the warnings, he doesn't find it a dreadful parish. He is young enough never to have known the church as a major part of community life, stimulated enough to find it a challenge, energetic enough to be always on the move. Apart from his involvement with Leybourne, he is padre to the Air Training Corps in Ditton and he is industrial chaplain at Reeds. Every Thursday morning he takes communion service for the Anglican Benedictine community of nuns at Malling Abbey. Leybourne and Malling Abbey are touchstones for his normal pastoral work; Leybourne because it is old-fashioned, the Abbey because to him it is a privilege. He loves this part of the week because he finds the Abbey a refreshing place to be, utterly marvellous. 'They've got their own kind of service and it's all sung and there are no musical instruments in the chapel at all so you have to pitch your own note and if you start on the wrong note you've had it, you're either going through the roof or falling through the floor.' At the Abbey he is in touch with the pulse of diocesan history. Bishop Gundulf built the Abbey on the land originally granted to his predecessor Buhric. Apart from the churches of East and West Malling, the Abbey had bestowed upon it the right to fairs and markets and, by Henry I, the right to all whales found in the bishopric of Rochester. The Abbey survived the Black Death of 1348, though two abbesses died in the year. It survived the casual dissolutions of the early sixteenth century by Wolsey and others, and the first major dissolution in 1536, because its income was more than £200 a year. But in 1538 Henry VIII caught up with it. Cromwell installed Margaret Vernon as Abbess. She had once been governess to his children and had been Abbess at a nunnery already dissolved. Now she was put into Malling to replace the less pliant Elizabeth Rede and she saw to her duty satisfactorily. She and her nuns were pensioned off, Vernon with £10 yearly, the eleven nuns with from £2.13s.4d. to £3 a year each.

In 1896 the Church of England bought back the Abbey from private owners and reconsecrated it for the Benedictines, who resumed the occupation so summarily interrupted by Henry Tudor. It is a closed order and outsiders may not walk among the cloisters. But the Revd Richard Lea is not an outsider, and every Thursday morning as he celebrates holy communion he feels the spirit upon him as bishops and abbesses and nuns here have since 1100.

Two typical days in the life of Richard Lea, taking Thursday as the starting point: He rises early, because the Abbey service is at 7.30. Back from
Malling, he retires to his cosily untidy study to write letters and prepare
for meetings. At ten he has a short service at Leybourne church. He does
not like midweek morning services because only a handful attend; but
when he took over as priest-in-charge part of the package was an old
curate who lives at Leybourne rectory and had always taken a Thursday
morning service. This week the curate is away, so Richard Lea takes the
service.

Back to his study until lunchtime with the family. After lunch he goes
down to Reed Medway Sacks between two and four o'clock. At four he
has an appointment at the Abbey. At five he chairs a meeting of Leybourne School managers that lasts until seven. From 7.30 until ten he
has a meeting of Holy Trinity parochial church council.

Next morning, Friday, he is getting dressed when his wife, who was up
before him, rushes in to say that the mother of one of their neighbours is
dying. She is a woman of nearly ninety. So he pops in there, says some
prayers with the family in the old lady's bedroom and promises to come
back later. Back home for breakfast. Then miscellaneous bits and pieces.
He is treasurer of the Tonbridge and Malling Volunteer Bureau which
he himself was instrumental in establishing. It is a central referral agency
for all sorts of useful voluntary and statutory welfare bodies. Anybody
who wants to help can telephone, anybody who wants to volunteer for
charity work can telephone to offer their services and be guided to the
right place. It is funded by the Kent county council Social Services
Department so it is carefully run, and since they have just had the annual
meeting, Richard Lea is, as he puts it, debriefing himself this morning.

Then he resumes writing a sermon. It's more than usually important
to get this sermon right because he is to deliver it on Saturday week at the
diocesan choirs festival at Rochester Cathedral: a big day for him. (On
the day, the Bishop of Tonbridge is there, and the Revd Richard Lea
preaches a sermon about unison and harmony choral singing. He favours
unison singing as a greater act of piety: harmony singing, he points out,
allows a lot of display to the greater glory of the individual than to that
of the Almighty. He quotes from a text by the German theologian Bonhoeffer, introducing him by waving a text above his head and making a
joke about 'my little red book'. It is a black joke within a bland joke:
Bonhoeffer was a radical whom the Nazis finally executed because he
refused to recant. Jokes are a well-known part of Richard Lea's armoury
— '*That* should be interesting', an East Malling parishioner remarked

sardonically when she heard that Richard Lea would be preaching in
Rochester — but if anyone expects his jokes to misfire in the massive
Romanesque solemnity of Rochester, they are mistaken. He is much
appreciated.) After working on the sermon, Richard Lea goes to Preston
Hall hospital in Aylesford to bring home an old man who lives just across
the lane from him. Then back to the sermon for the rest of the morning
and most of the afternoon.

Friday afternoons are usually a time for him to go out visiting, but
having given a lot of thought to the sermon he wants to get it down on
paper while it is fresh in his mind. Then he goes to the house of Pastor
Broad, the Lutheran who runs a group of six to a dozen people who work
in the village hall sorting through boxes of old spectacles, cleaning them
to send to hospitals and eye clinics, mostly in Africa and Asia. Richard
Lea manages after an hour of this to fit in one visit; and during the morning and again this afternoon he pops in to see Mrs Stephens, the old
woman who is dying. She is still alive when he goes to choir practice at
seven. That lasts until eight; and the next item in his diary is an interview with me. During our talk someone telephones him. Can he fit in
half an hour with the A.T.C. at Ditton on Wednesday week? He can't.
He already has a baptism visit arranged, a wedding interview, and a
meeting in Ryarsh village.

That is the normal pace of Richard Lea's days. Occasionally things
become more hectic. For the last six years he has produced the parish
magazine. He writes it, types it out once, types it again, this time on to
stencils, then runs it off. 'I do the whole thing myself. I have had help in
the past. It's only really three sheets of A4, but if I let somebody else type
the stencils as I did once it was illegible, and I mean this hasn't come out
all that brilliantly, but it's all quite reasonably set out, you see, and so I
take a pride in getting it right. This is issue number 77: I've done seventy-
seven of those, so I can now do it quite quickly, but at first it was more or
less a week's work to get that blooming thing done.

'So when I've got that and perhaps a couple of crucial sermons and
say a couple of people die . . . I mean, deaths: sometimes somebody dies
who lives on their own, there are no relations living here and all I've got
to do is go and take the service. No trouble. But it may be that there's
heavy mourning going on locally, you know, it's a very sad case, perhaps
it's a young mother or something like that, or it may be someone I
already knew very well and was closely involved with. Anyway. That
can mean daily visits, quite lengthy daily visits, particularly if I've been

involved or if it was a lengthy illness leading up to it. And sometimes in cases like that people do hang on to the clergy for support.'

Mr Lea plots his week fairly closely, but the unexpected throws the best-laid plans awry. Each Tuesday, Wednesday, and Thursday he has an evening meeting; sometimes two. Friday evening he usually has free. He is not free to go away at the week-ends, of course, but Saturdays and Sundays are easier days, though Sunday morning service is hard work, almost the way the theatre is for an actor.

'People often don't realise what physically hard work it is to take a service because you're on your feet the whole time and although you're not nervous in the way that someone who has never done it before would be, yet at the same time you're giving out. You're responsible for the whole thing and if it's going badly it's irritating, it can be very lowering. On the other hand if it's going very well and you come away feeling elated, that was super, there's a counter-effect in the evening. You know I find this so many times I expect it now, so I know if I come home and think, oh, super, I know that before I go to bed in the evening I shall feel fed up. It's cruel, you can't win.'

It's not that Richard Lea is bad at delegating; but he does feel that in Larkfield he has to keep pushing. Once he stops, the impetus falls off as well. Derek Chapman has had the opposite and gratifying experience in East Malling. When he arrived sixteen years ago he was expected, he says, to do everything. The parish stood or fell by the priest's ability to cope. And often, he says, the most godly priests are bad at coping. Now far more is done by the parish at large, principally by the parochial church council, which has sixteen members elected by the congregation, with a quarter retiring each year. In some ways this freedom of the P.C.C. to initiate policy is illusory; their decisions are always subject to the vicar's veto. 'Rightly or wrongly I act as chairman. This is different from synodical government where there's a lay chairman and a clerical chairman. The present set-up is that the incumbent has to take the chair even though he may be a very bad chairman. You may have a super chairman sitting beside you. Some people say that this sort of church government is still in its infancy. But it's encouraging that it's got so far. The church is rather conservative. Change doesn't come easily. Some people say we're trying to drag the church into the twentieth century.'

Daphne Chapman remarks that the congregation is more conservative than the clergy, and Derek Chapman agrees. By and large it is the con-

gregation who like what they've been used to, he says. But he takes his
hat off to them; they have put up with a lot.

The pace of change has accelerated in the Church of England during
Derek Chapman's time at East Malling, but it began before his incumbency. Even after the Second World War the congregation reflected
class hierarchy. The last lord of the manor died in 1937, but paternalism
had not altogether vanished. The Twisdens had had their own pew,
reached by a private door through the sacristy. In it they were concealed
from the vulgar gaze, though village talk had it that one Twisden at least
was supplied by his butler with sherry and biscuits to sustain him during
the sermon. After the war the congregation was still segregated by social
rank: the gentry sat at the front, the tradespeople in the middle, and the
workers (there were no longer any parishioners in service) at the back.
But the church's oak pews survived the twelfth and last baronet only a
decade or so; then they were discovered to be infested with deathwatch
beetle and were taken out and burnt; a loss to the appearance of the
building, but a gain in democracy. Movable raffia-seated chairs do not
for some reason lend themselves so easily to class distinctions.

The most important of the items the vicar and his council look after is
the church's budget. The end of titheing and the decline of the gentry
brought the church its biggest problem. Not ten miles away at Tudeley
the d'Avigdor Goldsmids of Somerhill House commissioned a complete
set of windows by Marc Chagall for the tiny parish church; and they paid
for a tunnel-vaulted marble ceiling in the nave. But patrons of this order
are an extreme rarity. Since the Twisden wealth was dissipated and the
Wigans ceased to be a power in the parish, East Malling has had none.
But Derek Chapman introduced to this parish the growing practice of
asking the congregation to pledge a part of its income annually to the
church. This takes the headache out of budgeting. People give what they
are able, and the church is able to anticipate its income and live within
its budget. The most expensive item is the fabric. The battlements of the
tower are crumbling and will have to be replaced. It will involve scaffold-
ing the tower, so it will cost £10,000 and will involve that last remedy,
reluctantly resorted to, a public appeal.

There have been two other appeals in the recent history of St James's.
The last one, in the early 1970s, was for the Decorated window in the
north aisle to be restored and refurbished with the fragments of glass
remaining from the Middle Ages and the Tudor period: one piece celebrates the connection of Hugh Catlyn with the parish (he who built the

battlements). The other appeal was in 1956, for £1,500 to repair the bell tower and rehang the bells.

The bells are as important to the church as the organ: some would say more so: they are the public manifestation of the glory of Christianity. When there is a wedding or a church service or a funeral or a royal Jubilee, the bells ring and the parish knows about it. Whether it cares or not is a different matter. The organist — at St James's, Daphne Chapman — is part of the service; the bell ringers in the big whitewashed chamber below the belfry are in a world of their own, kept in touch with the outside by the muffled sound of organ and choir through the ringing chamber floor, and by sight through the Norman slit window looking down into the churchyard where wedding parties prefer to have their photographs taken. And like waiters in the kitchen disparaging the diners in the restaurant or actors scorning critics or ballet dancers their audience, the ringers are liberated by their isolation to comment on those they serve. If Daphne Chapman muffs a chord, one of the ringers will say that she's playing with boxing gloves on. If a bride's nose is not retroussé, someone will compare it to Rudolph the Red-Nosed Reindeer. 'Never mind her; think of what their children will look like.' And so on the ringing chamber wall is a framed prayer to recall them to their duties:

> We beseech Thee, O Heavenly Father, to pour Thy grace into the hearts of those who work for Thee in ringing the bells of the church. Grant that we may never forget the sacredness of Thy House, nor profane it by thoughtlessness or irreverence; but make us ever mindful that, when we ring the bells we ring for Thy honour and glory; through Jesus Christ our Lord. Amen.

But bell ringers are not necessarily even numbered among the faithful. Many are: like Bob Garner, a world authority on tree grafting, now retired from the Research Station, but a member of the congregation and a bell ringer since his youth nearly half a century ago. Then there's young Stewart, still at school, and a member of the church choir as well: as soon as a wedding service is over and Daphne Chapman hits the first chords of the Wedding March, Stewart slips rapidly out of the church, holding his surplice clear of the floor with one hand, hurtles up the narrow spiral staircase into the tower, pulls the surplice off over his head, and seizes the red, white, and blue striped sally of one of the six ropes. Then the round begins.

East Malling had to reconstruct and re-train its ringing team after the ten years without bells, from 1956 to 1966, and they don't count themselves very skilful yet. They confine themselves to rounds and simple changes. The bell captain gives the nod, and his wife on the treble pulls evenly on her sally calling, 'Treble's going . . . she's gone.' Before the treble strikes the other ringers are pulling and the first round is under way, 1,2,3,4,5,6. Bob Garner's son, who is a bell ringer at Stansted in Essex, carries five thousand changes in his head. There's nothing as elaborate here, but after a few rounds the bell captain calls a change, and the order of the bells is varied: 1 2 3 4, 2 1 4 3 5 6, 3 1 2 4 5 6. The ringers are so adept at one change and do it so often that they sardonically call it among themselves East Malling Surprise.

Done properly, ringing is as precise as playing on a keyboard, and mysterious to watch because no ringer ever seems to break the even rhythm of his movement with the rope, yet as the bell captain calls the changes the order of the bells alters. Change ringing began in England and has never spread to the Roman Catholic lands or to Luther's or Calvin's. What the connection with the Reformation is, nobody knows, but change ringing started about then when bells began to be rehung in frames with heavy headstocks that enabled them to be turned upside down ready for ringing and then swung through very nearly a complete circle for each strike.

Sometimes the founders used to cast the bells in great pits in the churchyard, and there were bell founders' yards all over the country. In London, the centre of bell founding was Aldgate, at the eastern entrance to the City, and later, as City land grew more expensive, Whitechapel. At one time or another most of the churches of England and many of those areas of the world that used to be coloured pink on the map will have had dealings with the Whitechapel Bell Foundry, which is the greatest survivor of the foundries that devised the new way of hanging the bells. The Whitechapel Foundry started in 1583 when Robert Mot, master founder, moved his business there from Aldgate, where it had been since 1420 at least; and by amalgamations its history stretches back to 1270. When Whitechapel cast the Liberty Bell for the U.S. Bicentenary, it used precisely the same methods as for the original Liberty Bell made for Pennsylvania's fiftieth anniversary in 1752, and as for casting Big Ben on 10 April 1858, and for Westminster Abbey's bells in 1583 and 1598 (and for the replica set of the full peal of ten Abbey bells which was cast as a Bicentenary gift to the United States, but which still stands in the old Artichoke Inn yard at the foundry until somewhere can be found to hang them). Whitechapel cast Bow bells, and the oranges and lemons peal at St Clement Danes, and the bells of Wren's St Lawrence Jewry. In 1662 Antony Bartlet, the master founder, cast six bells for Samuel Pepys's parish church in Hart Street, St Olave's; and three decades later his son James cast five bells for East Malling; Thomas Mears made the sixth, the treble, in 1831. Once tuned, the bells are good for two, three, four hundred years, half a millennium and more. Occasionally, as the clapper wears the bell metal thin, the bell will be quarter-turned. James Bartlet's bells hung in East Malling for two hundred years before being given their first quarter-turn.

When the East Malling ringers have finished in the tower (apart from religious engagements, they practise for half an hour every Thursday evening), they reconnect the 12-hundredweight tenor bell to the clock to strike the hours. And the ringers hitch another length of rope to the spare piece beneath the sally, so that it may hang through a hole in the bell-ringing chamber to the ground floor, for the verger to summon the faithful to service — those dedicated folk who run stalls at the fêtes, collect for jumble sales, act as sidesmen, make the floral arrangements, and, at harvest festival, bring the produce of their gardens to the church as an offering.

**There is perhaps no class of dwellings so pleasing as the rural seats of the English gentry.** Macaulay, The History of England

*Ham Mill Mead from Walter's maps of the Twisden Estate*

Ham-Mill Meads

These Foure Meadows, are in Sr Thomas Twisden's Owne Occupation And containe as Followeth:

| | | Acres | Roods or Yards | Perches or Rods |
|---|---|---|---|---|
| | | Ac: | R: | P: |
| A | Catts Mead is | 02 | 0 | 09 |
| B | Cobbs Mead is | 04 | 2 | 05 |
| C | The Nine Yards | 02 | 0 | 33 |
| D | Stretfields Mead | 02 | 1 | 39 |
| | The Total Sum is | 11 | 1 | 06 |

When Sir John Ramskill Twisden died in 1937, old, blind, and unmarried, his house was falling down around him. The floor was collapsing
into the cellar, the rooms were damp, the plaster peeling. There was no
electricity. The lake was overgrown with reeds. The stables and the
empty tithe barn were ruinous with neglect. It was, said the builder who
came to restore it, a poor man's mansion.

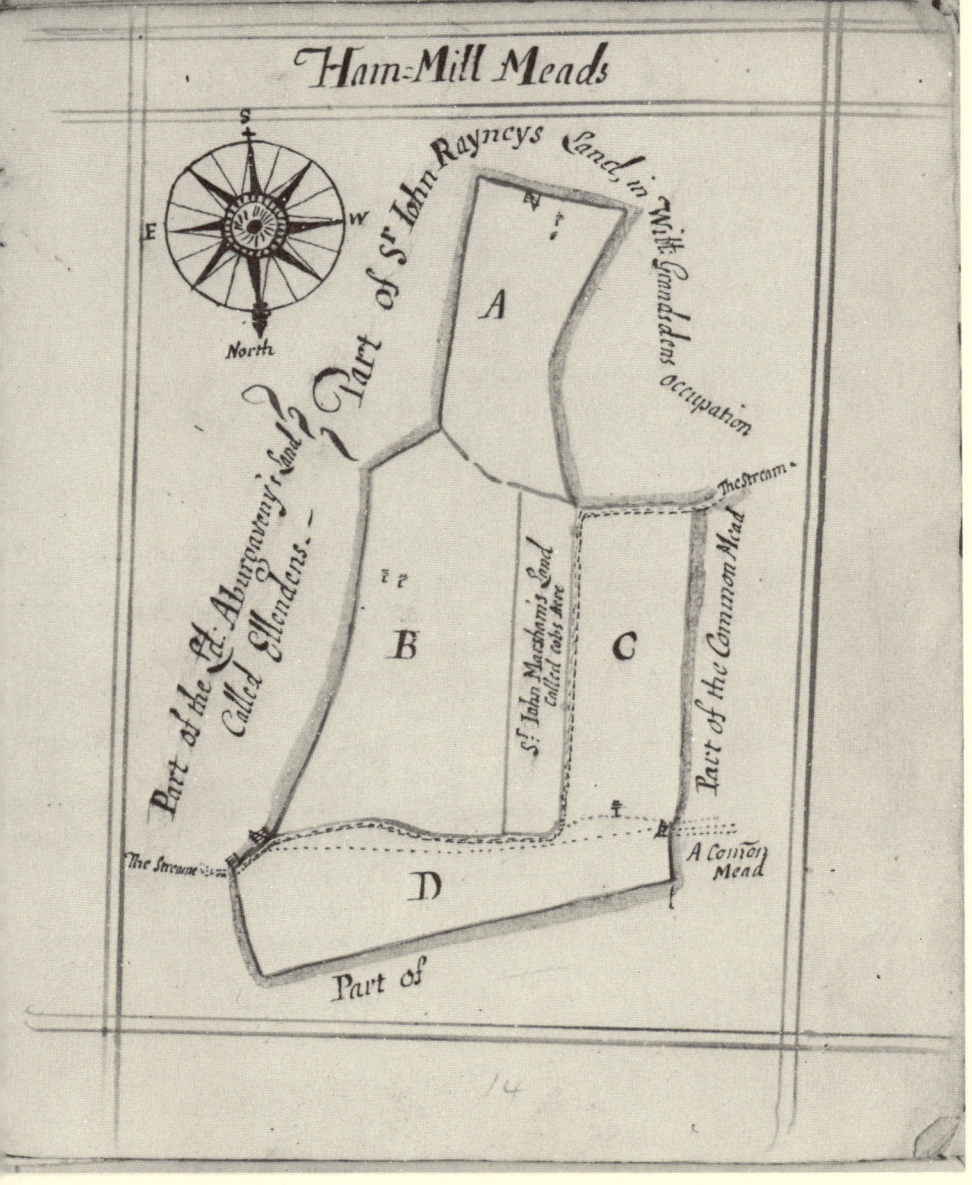

Sir John's unmarried sister, Catherina Martha, had died some years before. He had a small domestic staff (today, the vicar's wife's daily remembers receiving 6s.8d. a week as chambermaid at Bradbourne), but it was a shadow of the years when a butler, footmen, a cook, kitchen staff, scullery maid, housekeeper, chambermaids, valet, coachman, groom, stable boys, gardeners, laundry maids, and steward had run the Twisden household. Every evening a schoolgirl walked to Bradbourne from her house in the High Street to read the headlines from *The Times* to Sir John. And it was in *The Times* of 9 November 1937 that his death notice appeared: 'Sir John Ramskill Twisden, 12th and last Baronet of Brad-bourne, in his 81st year.'

It was the end not just for him, nor for the Twisdens, but for a whole class. Today Linton Place, the home of Walpole's friend Robert Mann, is a school. In 1978 the Style family of Wateringbury sold Wateringbury Place, the family home for four hundred years. Roydon Hall at East Peckham, once the home of the senior branch of the Twisden family, is the Maharishi's capital of Transcendental Meditation. An Earl of West-morland raised Mereworth Castle, and of that noble Palladian villa Christopher Smart wrote:

> Nor shalt thou, Mereworth, remain unsung,
> Where noble Westmorland, his country's friend,
> Bids British greatness love the silent shade,
> Where piles superb, in classic elegance,
> Arise, and all is Roman, like his heart.

Now the castle is the country seat of His Excellency Sayed Mohammed Mahdi Al-Tajir, Ambassador Extraordinary and Plenipotentiary in London of the United Arab Emirates. And Bradbourne is the head-quarters of East Malling Research Station.

The old families have passed and left scarcely more trace in the fabric of England than the Romans did. In two hundred years the industrial revolution has swept them away and with them a whole way of life and the system of patronage that had survived unscathed almost since Mealla's tribe settled the nearly 3,000 acres of land beside the Medway, and that cemented village social relations for better, for worse. In the round, the history of the gentry is the history of the shaping influence on England. Through trade and land ownership and the study of the law, the gentry became the power behind the throne and, more to the point, the power that kept the throne and the overweening aristocracy in its

Tending the orchards: (*above*) frost-fighting in 1935;
(*below*) grass-cutting in 1979

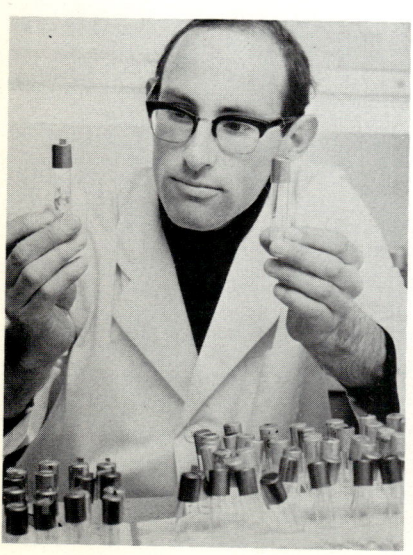

(*above*) hop-pickers at Heath Farm;
(*below*) East Malling Research Station: until the mid-1970s
the horse and test-tube worked side by side

(*above*) Clare House; (*below*) Bradbourne, once the manor house
and now the East Malling Research Station

Broadwater

constitutional place. In East Malling in the time of Elizabeth and the early Stuarts, the Manninghams were merchants and lawyers, and after them, the Twisdens were lawyers again and Members of Parliament, their second sons soldiers and sailors, their third sons churchmen. On their own demesne, as successors in their manors to the thegns of Saxon times, and, at the Reformation, to the lands and tithes and jurisdiction of the Church, the gentry held enormous power and patronage.

Riding the gathering wave that swept feudalism away, Henry II had created Justices of the Peace to curtail some of the *ad hoc* powers of the lords of the manor, and indeed the powers of the Court Baron dwindled. But lord of the manor or Justice of the Peace, Member of Parliament or freeman of the City of Rochester, the names were the same and few could deny them.

And yet probably Sir John was not unhappy at the passing of power. He was an antiquarian who had succeeded in untangling the skein of his family's last troubled years, marked by intrigue, envy, skulduggery, vaulting ambition, cheating, and hot-headed wilfulness. Sir John had launched an action in the high court of England, one that caught the public interest very much as the action of the Tichborne claimant did, but with this difference: Sir John steered his case to success. And that meant that in his blood ran the blood of the Finches and the Roydons and the Wyatts: Wyatt the rebel and Wyatt the poet. It ran thinly, but it ran. The Wyatts, the Fanes, the Colepeppers, my lord of Abergavenny, my lord of Westmorland: these had been names of honour and privilege in Kent and a power in the whole of England. And the Twisdens had married among them and were fit to sit among them in history, and he, Sir John, the last of the Twisdens, had set the record straight.

When the first Twisden, Thomas, started buying land in East Malling in 1643, he came as a second son; an ambitious second son, but not the potential head of a family. Yet he was already wearing his name with a difference. His father and older brother, of Roydon Hall, spelt the family name with a *y*, as Twysdens had always done since the yeoman Adam de Twysden had been possessed of the manor of Twysenden in the deepest Weald.

Thomas Twisden was a barrister, and a successful one. He became serjeant-at-law in 1654, but the year before, the manor court rolls for East Malling show, he had established himself in style: 'Alienaro Ann et Rici Manningham Thome Twisden the capital messuage of Bradbourne.' The Ann and Richard Manningham who sold Bradbourne to Thomas Twisden were the descendants of John Manningham the diarist, who watched in the City of London on 24 March 1602, as King James VI of Scotland was proclaimed King of England: 'No tumult, no contradicion, noe disorder in the city; every man went about his busines, as readlie, as peaceably, as securely, as though there had bin noe change, nor any newes ever heard of competitors. God be thanked, our king hath his right!' And one of those who conducted the king from Scotland to the capital of his new sceptred realm was Thomas Twisden's father, William. James rewarded William, first with a knighthood and then, when he created the order in 1611, with a baronetcy.

Thomas's older brother was Roger, a scholar famed in his time: 'the learned Sir Roger Twysden', as John Evelyn wrote in his diary after meeting him about the billeting of Dutch prisoners of war. It was clear to Thomas Twisden that if he were to make a mark in his own right, he must move from Roydon Hall. He was a man for all seasons, and Bradbourne brought him luck.

There was one stumble, but it can have done him no harm in the eyes of Charles II: in 1653 Serjeant Twisden defended George Coney, a citizen of London who had refused to pay a duty on the grounds that it had been imposed without the authority of Parliament. Oliver Cromwell knew Coney and tried to persuade him to pay. Coney was a staunch Puritan and Cromwellian, but a stauncher Parliamentarian, and he refused. Cromwell had him arrested. Serjeant Twisden applied for a writ of habeas corpus, and compared the committal of Coney with Star Chamber proceedings. The Protector was infuriated. He summoned Twisden and Coney's two other advocates, Serjeant Maynard and Mr Wadham Wyndham, to a Council of State.

There, Cromwell committed the three advocates to the Tower for uttering words tending to sedition and subversion. Their authority in court, Cromwell said, derived from him; lawyers must not be suffered to prate what it would not become them to hear. Maynard and Wyndham apologised and were released from the Tower. Twisden pleaded that sedition could not have been further from his thoughts and that his health and need to support a wife and eleven children (all living: this was Kentish yeoman stock) made freedom imperative. He too was released. Coney faced up to the realities of power, submitted to Cromwell, and went free.

While Thomas Twisden licked his wounds, his brother-in-law Matthew Thomlinson rode high as a colonel-of-horse in the New Model Army. He had joined the Parliamentary forces in 1642, and on their victory was nominated to the bench to try the defeated king. He opted out, but accepted the commission to guard the king between his arrest and his trial and execution. His courtesy made him a pleasant companion for the king, and on his way to the scaffold Charles rewarded Thomlinson with the *memento mori* of a gold toothpick.

Thomlinson rose to sit among the highest in the land: he was a member of the Council of State, but avoided sitting in judgement on Thomas Twisden over the Coney case because he was out of the country as a member of the Lord-Lieutenant of Ireland's Council. And in 1657 Oliver Cromwell's puppet ruler in Ireland, his fourth son Henry Cromwell, knighted Matthew Thomlinson. In 1659 the restored Long Parliament made Thomlinson one of the five Commissioners for the Civil Government of Ireland.

The first blow fell later that same year. Thomlinson was arrested for 'too great an inclination to the side of the Army'. In January 1660, he was impeached, but allowed to return to England. There, the Commonwealth was in ruins. Oliver Cromwell was dead. Richard Cromwell had resigned as Protector. General Monck, soldier and pragmatist, agreed to the restoration of Stuart rule. Sir Matthew — how hollowly the title rang — could not have been worse off facing impeachment in Ireland. His seat of Ampthill Park was taken away and restored to the royalist ejected under Cromwell. He faced trial as an accomplice in the death of Charles I.

As Thomlinson's fortunes fell, Twisden's rose. On 22 June, within a month of the king's return, Charles reappointed the serjeants-at-law, and on 2 July Thomas Twisden took the oath as a Judge of the King's Bench. In his own laconic account, '. . . on the second day of July 1660, I was sworne one of Judges of ye Kings Bench, and the same day in the afternoone, I, together with my brother Atkyns, were, by my Lord Chancelour, carried to the King at Whitehal, by whom we were both then knighted.'

In October Twisden sat on the Bench at the Old Bailey in the trial of the regicides. After some argument, his brother-in-law Matthew Thomlinson had not been charged, but instead turned king's evidence. Thomlinson insisted that he had never taken part in the proceedings against King Charles I. Some royalists argued that even so, as the king's guard, Thomlinson ought to have allowed Charles to escape: in the end, Charles's own commendation of Thomlinson to his son, now Charles II, carried the day.

Sir Thomas went from fame to fame. He took part in the trial of Sir Harry Vane (convicted and executed for treason against Charles II) and of John James, the Puritan zealot (convicted and executed for preaching treason). He had several court encounters with the redoubtable George Fox, founder of the Quakers, the last of which left Fox imprisoned for a year in Lancaster and Scarborough castles to expunge, in effect, contempt. But the case in which Sir Thomas showed the irascible streak in his character which marked so many of his descendants (and brought their fortunes tumbling) was the appeal of John Bunyan in the Swan Inn, Bedford, against his imprisonment after trial at Bedford quarter-sessions in January 1661.

Bunyan was charged under a statute of Elizabeth I which had been re-enacted under Charles II, that enjoined prison, transportation, or death for dissenters. It was, in short, a serious matter. Bunyan argued that the statute was not intended to apply to private meetings. On conviction, he appealed to the midsummer assizes. His wife Elizabeth tried without success to petition Judge Hale, who was thought to be soft on dissent. The next day she threw a petition into the coach of Judge Twisden. He angrily told her that Bunyan would not go free until he promised not to preach. At the hearing in the Swan Inn, Elizabeth again took John Bunyan's part: 'He preacheth nothing but the word of God,' she said.

'He preach the word of God!' said Judge Twisden. 'He runneth up and down, and doth harm.'

'No, my Lord, it's not so, God hath owned him, and done much good by him.'

'God! His doctrine is the doctrine of the Devil.'

'My Lord, when the righteous judge shall appear, it will be known, that his doctrine is not the doctrine of the Devil.'

The appeal was lost. Bunyan served twelve years. And in 1666 the king created Thomas first baronet of Bradbourne.

This was the year of the Great Fire of London, and Twisden's last service to the nation. After the fire, he sat with the Barons of the Exchequer, the Justices of the Common Plea, and the Judges of the King's Bench to arbitrate on the boundaries of the property — mostly built of wood — which had been obscured. For this function the city granted £792 in payment to Joseph Michael Wright, Lely's only major British-born rival, for painting the portraits of all twenty-two arbitrators to hang in the Guildhall, where they remain today.

But by now Sir Thomas was old, out-of-date, and exhausted. He had learned his law in the reign of James I and too many changes had happened since. He didn't want to go but in 1678 he reluctantly agreed to step down from the Bench in exchange for a pension of £500 a year — half his salary — and the right to call himself Judge Twisden for life. Locally, he had bought from Sir John Rayney (a baronet whose fortunes had run out) the lordship of the manor.

Two years before Sir Thomas's retirement, the king granted him one more favour. When Sir Thomas first moved into Bradbourne the coach road from Larkfield to the middle of East Malling ran past his front door. The judge himself was busy and probably anyway not too much worried by this diminution in his style, but he stood in good stead at the court and there cannot have been much doubt about the outcome when his son acted for him in the matter of diverting one of the king's highways. At any rate, the king granted his charter:

> Charles the second, by the grace of God, King of England, Scotland, France and Ireland, defender of the faith, etc, to all to whom these present letters shall come, greetings. Since by a certain inquisition taken by our order at East Malling in our county of Kent on the 6th day of December in the year of our reign the twenty-seventh, by the oath of worthy and lawful men of that county, it has been found that it will not be to our or other's harm, damage or prejudice, if we grant to Roger Twisden of East Malling aforesaid, esquire, that he may enclose a certain highway which runs between East Malling Crosse and Larkfield in the said parish of East Malling and may have the power to keep it so inclosed for himself and his heirs for ever. On condition that he the aforesaid Roger Twisden makes in place of that way a certain other way of the same length and breadth on the soil of the said Roger sufficient for those traversing the same way as by the inquisition aforesaid, remaining as of record in the court of our Chancery more fully appears.
>
> Know now that we, of our special grace and from our certain knowledge and sole initiative have granted and given licence . . . to the aforesaid Roger Twisden that he may stop up and enclose the said way and may have the power to keep it so stopped up and enclosed to himself and his heirs and assigns without hindrance from us our heirs or successors or any justices, escheators, sheriffs or other bailiffs or servants of us or others whatsoever. . . .

There remained to divert a footpath and the park was complete and private, stretching from Larkfield to the church, and from New Road (as it remains to this day) to Ditton.

Finally, Sir Thomas had furnished a family vault beneath the nave of St James's, a former bone-house of which the Archbishop of Canterbury noted, in granting a licence for its new service, 'no use has been made within the memory of Man'. Sir Thomas's body was the first to be laid to rest there. He died on 2 January 1683.

No other Twisden would reach such eminence, but the family fortunes were to flourish until deep trouble set in at the succession of the fifth baronet, Sir Roger. On the face of it he was a bluff Squire Western. He kept a pack of hounds and had his portrait painted in his park in hunting pink. When a tenant took his hat off to speak to him, Sir Roger snapped: 'Put thy hat on thy head, man, or I'll break it with my staff.' But there was a long tradition of learning in this family and the management of an estate and the conduct of business as an M.P. and a captain of militia was not for the sort of buffoon portrayed by Fielding. Sir Roger was, in addition, a D.C.L. of Oxford University. But he had the irascible streak characteristic of the Twisdens, and it showed itself with dire consequences for the fortunes of his family.

Gentry came and gentry went, but as a class in the '60s and '70s of the eighteenth century they were not threatened. And the Twisdens had not, like many, overreached themselves in rebuilding Bradbourne; in fact the sixth baronet was able to improve it further by rebuilding the south front with a sumptuous bow window. The trouble arose because Sir Roger's younger son William was, in the old-fashioned phrase, a ne'er-do-well, and when he contracted what his family regarded as an unsuitable marriage — indeed, would not recognise as a marriage at all — Sir Roger disinherited him.

When Sir Roger's eldest son died with only a daughter, Rebecca, his youngest son, the Reverend John Papillon Twisden, inherited Bradbourne. But Bradbourne was not enough. Acting on the family pretence that his disinherited brother William's son John was illegitimate, he took the title.

He was unable to enjoy his guilty usurpation. In the first place he felt badly about cheating his nephew. He put him through school and later, like his father, into the navy. In the second place, John Papillon inherited only the house: his niece Rebecca inherited the park and the furnishings of Bradbourne. And when she reached her majority John Papillon had by the settlement to pay her £10,000, something he could do only by selling land.

The gentry of England were riding high. They controlled the Commons, they waxed rich on the newly efficient agriculture on their demesne lands and their freshly enclosed fields, and they drew impressive rents from their tenants; some discovered new wealth in the coal seams beneath their land. But in East Malling there was no coal, there was only waste land to enclose, and such meadow, arable, and orchard as lay in the possession of the heir to Bradbourne now had to go. The rich patrimony that Judge Twisden had put together not much more than a century before was falling apart.

Rebecca had married Thomas Law Hodges, a brilliant young man, formerly captain of Harrow School, a barrister who began his studies at Lincoln's Inn at the age of seventeen, a Whig Member of Parliament for Kent, a freeman of the City of Rochester, an improving landlord — one of the landowners who comes well out of J. L. and Barbara Hammond's classic of labour history, *The Village Labourer*. But land then was liable to corrupt its owners in the way that capital can now.

Hodges affected the Twisden belief that William Twisden's son John was a bastard. Perhaps he really did believe it. Either way, what he now did was not quite what the chaps would expect of a former captain of Harrow. On 2 January 1841, Purton, the Bradbourne coachman, arrived with the news that the last baronet had died. Hodges travelled to Bradbourne and, in the absence of John Twisden (by now a retired naval captain), he spent all day burning papers in a fire in the library that became, as Purton reported the footman saying, 'so wonderfully hot that "the heat seemed to come against him when he opened the door."' Sir John had apparently expressed the desire that Captain John Twisden should inherit Bradbourne, but the evidence was contradictory and if the baronet had not died intestate, Hodges must have thought, he was certainly intestate now.

Somehow, however, a draft will survived, and this was taken as conclusive. Bradbourne was Captain Twisden's. He had inherited a shell. His life had taught him to be practical, and though he thought himself to be the rightful baronet as well, he wrote in later years in answer to an enquiry from the editor of the *New Baronetage*: 'I am a retired officer of the Royal Navy and being upwards of 75 years of age seclusion and quiet are more agreeable to me than the assumption of a title my property is too small to support.'

It was a matter-of-fact approach to life. The Roydon Hall branch of the Twisdens had meanwhile failed more spectacularly. Mixed up in the

gay life of the court of George III, a succession of spendthrifts and
gamblers went through thousands of pounds of capital. One younger son,
who became Bishop of Raphoe, in Armagh, was shot dead at Wrotham
Heath; by a highwayman, the family said, but the evidence suggests that
he himself was the highwayman attempting to rob his brother's house
guest of the previous evening. The bishop's daughter married Lord
Jersey and became the Prince of Wales's mistress. The Twysden estates
had to be sold, even Roydon Hall itself, and one Twysden had to earn his
living as a porter at Wateringbury station on the railway line opened in
1844 between Tonbridge and Maidstone. But it took three generations
of Twysdens to bring their fortunes to that pass. The bluff Sir Roger
wrecked the Twisdens of Bradbourne with one ill-conceived will.

There it might have remained except that John Ramskill Twisden, a
descendant of Captain Twisden, developed an obsession with proving
the family line. If John Ramskill was right, his father, who was still alive,
was *de jure* eleventh baronet. His father reluctantly agreed to act his part
in the claim, but the only way Captain John could be proved a legiti-
mate son of William Twisden was if a grandchild still living petitioned
the Probate, Divorce and Admiralty Division in the Law Courts.

This was 1909. William's marriage was presumed to have taken place
sometime in the early 1760s. Yet nearly 150 years later there was a living
grandchild: Captain John Twisden's sole surviving daughter. Without
Emily the petition would be lost irretrievably. She had been born in 1813
and was in her ninety-sixth year.

The case of Emily Henrietta Twisden versus the Attorney General
opened on the morning of Friday, 18 June 1909, before Mr Justice
Bargrave Deane. The press had a field day the following morning. All the
world loves a peer, but a baronet will do nearly as well.

There was no marriage certificate, but there was one piece of evidence
supporting the Twisden case. The usurping John Papillon Twisden had
befriended both John Larking, the man who had bought so much of his
land, and the vicar of East Malling, Samuel Godmond, and it was to
both of these that he confessed his belief in his nephew's legitimacy. They
in turn told Larking's son, Lambert Larking, who felt, as he put it, 'an
*indescribable* interest in this irregular and almost romantic tale'. And
Lambert Larking had written many years later, in 1863, to a son of
Captain Twisden setting out the facts as he knew them:

Ryarsh Vicarage
21st October 1863

My dear Sir,

I am exceedingly glad that you have, in kind confidence, opened the subject of the cruel wrong which has been done you as it will enable me to recall for your use a large amount of circumstantial coincidence which ought to be preserved. . . .

My father first inspired me with interest on the subject before he built Clare House, and when he was living in the Rectory (now occupied by Mr Wimble) he was a most attached friend of your great uncle Sir John Papillon Twisden — in daily and almost hourly intercourse — so much so that Sir John had made a little door of communication between the Rectory garden and the park of which each had the key. My father has often lingered over his conversations with Sir John on the position which he had assumed, as heir and Baronet — a position he never ceased to say that he felt he had no right to assume — that it was robbing his nephew (your father) — that it pressed sorely on his conscience, and yet he knew not how to relieve himself. It was an incessant subject of lamentation in his conversation (all this I have again and again heard from my father). He was never at ease — and, in his latter days, entirely secluded himself from society. . . . He had a little covered rest on a mound inside the park at the corner of Larkfield road, in which a little window was cut through which he could peep at the passing world, while he was himself unseen — and at Church, which he reached by his private door, he used to be curtained in. . . .

There followed more of similar substance, and then the subject switched to the Revd S. F. Godmond: '. . . he expressed to Mr Godmond the Vicar of East Malling, his conviction that his brother William's son was legally born and the rightful heir — that he made the remainders of his will in accordance . . . he always deemed himself a usurper.'

The Judge read this letter overnight and on the second day of the hearing, he announced: 'I will reserve judgment.'

Counsel for Emily Twisden was instantly on his feet. 'The petitioner is very old, and she is the last surviving grandchild of William and Mary Twisden,' he pointed out delicately. 'May I suppose that your lordship could date your judgment from today?'

'I do not know about that,' the Judge said. 'But I think there can be no

danger now. The fact that I am reserving judgment now will not preju-
dice you in any way.'

They need not have worried. The court did not reconvene until 5 July,
but Emily was still alive, and the Judge found in her favour.

The baronetcy supposed lapsed in 1841 was alive. Burke's *Peerage and
Baronetage* would need a revived and rewritten entry. Captain John
Twisden, who had never wanted the recognition, was *de jure* seventh
baronet of Bradbourne from 4 October 1779. John Ramskill Twisden's
father was the eleventh baronet.

It was a triumph, of sorts. An antiquarian's triumph. The baronetcy
itself had no meaning. Captain John knew that when his cousin died in
1841. From the time of Judge Twisden for nearly two centuries, the
gentry owned more than half the land of England, leaving the crown and
the aristocrats, the Church and yeoman farmers to split the rest. In 1880
cheap imports of food from abroad for the first time in history knocked
the bottom out of land as an investment, but long before then the Twisden
finances had dwindled. Elsewhere in England handsome rents from the
railway boom revived flagging fortunes, but when the London, Chatham
and Dover Railway built a line through New Hythe, the Twisdens
received nothing: and even the vicar's cash in lieu of tithes yielded precisely £2.5s.9d. The 1832 Reform Bill weakened the power of the squire-
archy nationally; in 1889 the Local Government Act created county
councils and ended local domination as well. Anything but the shadow
of Twisden power and patronage had passed from the parish. True, the
manor court struggled on into the middle of the nineteenth century,
quaintly extracting the ancient forms of fealty to the lord of the manor.
But since the paper and corn mills had ceased to be small yeoman-run
enterprises, the fealty of villagers had passed in fact if not fiction to the
mill owners, the men who built them their terrace cottages up the east
side of High Street and along the west end of Mill Street.

One privilege the Twisdens did keep. They remained the impro-
priators of the great tithes, the tithes which had been wrested from the
Abbey at the dissolution and passed down from Thomas Cranmer until
they reached Judge Twisden. So Sir John Ramskill Twisden, when in
1914 he took his rightful place as twelfth baronet, was able to dictate what
alterations should or should not take place in the chancel of St James's.
And in 1920 Sir John prevented the widow of a soldier killed in action
from putting up a memorial to her husband; the fellow may have been a

hero, but the family was hardly East Malling stock, *after* all. And as he lay dying, he refused to allow the deathwatch-beetle-ridden pews to be removed from the chancel. It was not a glorious chapter.

As for the principal players in the drama of the previous century, Rebecca Hodges died two years after losing the battle for Bradbourne and her husband, political to the last, described her on her tombstone as 'the last of the Twisdens'. He himself died in 1857 and his children erected a memorial tablet in his praise: '. . . faithful in every relation of public & private life.' And Lambert Larking died in 1868 shortly before the publication of his great edition of *The Domesday Book of Kent*. His own memorial is an entry in the *Dictionary of National Biography* celebrating his scholarship: his last act of piety was to fill a double lancet in East Malling with stained glass to the memory of his father, John Larking. The window depicted the Return of Lazarus, and Lost Sheep Found.

# 4 Clene, swete, holsom alpha acid

**What busy bustling labouring scenes now mark the harvest morn.**   John Clare, 'The Harvest Morning'

*Broadwater Farm from Walter's maps of the Twisden Estate*

TWO MEETINGS WITH Fred Stanley. The first, a Sunday morning, late September, after a night of high winds. Half his apple and pear crop is on the ground, which means that he won't be able to sell it. He is depressed, talking of the indifferent recognition given to farmers by the nation. Broadwater, his farm, may have to give up fruit. And the market for hops is unpredictable.

| Names & Contents | Ac: R: P: |
|---|---|
| A: The Houſe yards & Hemplott | 01 — 0 — 06 |
| B: The Meadow Spott | 00 — 3 — 09 |
| C: Springet hill Field | 09 — 3 — 00 |
| D: Dickly | 09 — 1 — 32 |
| E: The Home Field | 17 — 1 — 14 |
| F: Crooked Field | 05 — 3 — 00 |
| G: Vpper 4: Acre Field | 04 — 2 — 32 |
| H: Inner Louelocks | 04 — 1 — 14 |
| I: Outer Louelocks | 03 — 2 — 03 |
| K: Quarry Field | 03 — 3 — 10 |
| L: Six Acre Field | 06 — 3 — 18 |
| M: Barn Field | 12 — 0 — 16 |
| N: Waterdowne Bottom | 02 — 1 — 00 |
| O: Waterdown hill | 05 — 2 — 16 |
| P: Beers Field | 03 — 0 — 02 |
| Q: Beers Wood | 01 — 2 — 00 |
| Summe of Acres | 92 — 00 — 20 |

*Note, that thoſe Boundary lines in this Mapp which are Pricked on the Outſide are Fences not maintained by this Land but by such as bound against it on the otherside*

*Quere Whither the Hedg (37) belong to, this Farm or to, Esqr Honywood is in Dispute by the Tenants*

The second meeting, September again, a couple of years later. It is soon after 7.30 one midweek morning. There is plenty of dew and Fred Stanley is wearing a pale windcheater to keep out the early nip. But the sky is clear blue and the sun is already riding high. The first freshly picked and sorted hops of the day are arriving on the oast platform outside at first-floor level. They are ready for spreading out and drying on the floor of the kiln. It is not going to be a good harvest this season, but Fred Stanley is exhilarated by the bustle. It is the high point of the year.

For the outsider too this is the prettiest sight in farming. The oast building is a large brick rectangle with four cylindrical kilns and their conical tiled roofs capped by white wooden cowls each with a tail on which BROADWATER is picked out in neat black capital letters. Inside, the oast floor measures about seventy-five feet by fifty feet; pitched roof with heavy wooden beams and tiles without a ceiling, unplastered whitewashed brick walls, brick piers one side, cast iron another. Along two sides of the floor are the double doors, seven feet by seven feet, for each kiln.

One pair of doors stands open now. The drier and his assistant are preparing to shovel the hops off the kiln floor. Man and boy, they have been here all night. They have two iron bedsteads downstairs on the ground floor in what looks like an N.C.O.s' bunk room. A kettle, a brown teapot, a pint of milk half drunk, an electric grill, a paperback: *Rommel, My Part in His Downfall*. The drier arrived on a Suzuki motorbike, his assistant on an orange BSA racing bicycle. Both machines lean against the wall outside the bunk room. The drier and his mate take it in turns to snatch some sleep while the hops dry. For three weeks, this room will be their home.

Down here on the ground floor are the oil furnaces that throw up heat through the wooden lattice-work of the drying floor above. And there is a little tray of burning sulphur to keep the hops green as they dry out. That is traditional. In 1485, before hop growing had become an industry (the usually accepted date for that is 1524), beer brewers received orders to use only 'gode, clene, sweete, holsom and greyne hoppes'. The alpha acid in hops is what gives the hoppy flavour to beer, not the greenness. But buyers still like hops to look the colour of new banknotes, so that's what they get.

The hops in the kiln are spread a foot thick across the circular net that covers the wide floor. The nets used to be horsehair, now they are goat hair and they cost £500 each. You can buy them made of nylon for half the price, but they curl at the edges. When the driers spread the hops across the floor with wide wooden spatula-like shovels, they bury two thermometers at different depths. With the doors shut, the furnace blasting heat upwards, a ballpoint pen fitted to a gauge on the wall starts marking a time/temperature graph. The line climbs swiftly for half an hour from 70° Fahrenheit to 135° and then after forty minutes levels out at about 140° Fahrenheit. When the differential temperature between the hops at the top of the heap and those at the bottom holds steady, the hops are something like ready. That will be in maybe six hours' time.

But now at eight in the morning one kiln-load of hops is dried and being pressed into pockets: long bags of jute and polythene suspended through a hole in the floor. The pockets stretch half as long again under the pressure of 1½ hundredweight of dried hops forced into them by the ancient cast-iron machine made by W. Weeks, Agricultural Machine Makers, of Maidstone. The firm is long gone, but they made their engine to last with the pride of a nation on which the sun would never set. The hop press is converted now to electricity and by the end of this season's harvest it will have crushed 240 fragrant hundredweight of hops into 160 bags. And each 1½ hundredweight of dried hops represents 8 hundredweight of hops fresh from the hop ground: the loss is all water. Once, the hop drier had to wind the hop press down by hand, eight or nine times to a pocket, and in the days when Charles Mercer built a fruit and hop empire based on Broadwater there was one miraculous harvest of 1,429 pockets of hops: maybe 12,000 laborious hand-cranking operations of Mr Weeks's machine.

But that was in 1901, when 120 acres of Broadwater were hop garden (today it is 28). These were years of prosperity which fed Charles Mercer's land hunger. For a while, starting in the era of high farming in the second half of the nineteenth century, the Mercers had been the biggest landowners in East Malling. Their holdings dwarfed the Twisdens, and John Larking at the height of his wealth, and the Wigans. Charles Mercer farmed Broadwater and its neighbour Heath Farm, where he raised pheasants for sport. He bought Borough Court farm, a sub-manor in Ditton, where the Twisdens had once held sway, and Cobdown Farm, and New Barns, in West Malling, on Broadwater's western flank. He rented a hundred acres of Sir John Twisden's land at Bradbourne, from the church to the London Road and east to the boundaries with Ditton, and the hops he grew there he dried at the oasts in Mill Street that have become offices for a cut-price furniture warehouse. Once this Bradbourne hop ground had been the demesne farm of the lords of the manor, and then their deer park; and they had owned

Broadwater and leased it out. Now it was the tenant who owned Broadwater and called the tune at Bradbourne while the last baronet sat marooned in his mouldering mansion. And Charles Mercer owned West Malling cricket field, where W. G. Grace had played for All England against the Men of Kent and Dickens set the Dingley Dell and All Muggleton match (or so they say who have studied the Boz illustration).

But the prime years which yielded the money for this land never returned. In earlier wars, villagers had expected to lose men called to the colours. But the Great War was serious: Mr Asquith was calling up horses. Broadwater had nine horses requisitioned. Only the year before Mrs Mercer had saved Rufus and Beauty, the family's coach horses, from a fire that consumed the oast and their stable beneath (Charles Mercer, at a meeting in West Malling, heard the news and got home on his bicycle before the fire brigade could find horses to harness to the fire engine). Now even Rufus and Beauty went to serve their country, though one of the pair was back soon at Preston Hall Blue Cross hospital in Aylesford, wounded in combat but covered in glory.

In 1917 Lord Ernle's Board of Agriculture ordered Charles Mercer to grub half Broadwater's acreage of hops and grow corn to fill hungry bellies with bread instead of beer. The great years of the hops never returned, and in 1926, the year of his death, Charles Mercer sold the whole estate except for Heath Farm.

In the Second World War, with the last baronet dead now for five years, East Malling Research Station bought Bradbourne and its tithe barn and stables; and the hundred acres that Charles Mercer's son John was farming. And three decades later the wind that blew Fred Stanley's apples off his trees blew down a new hop garden up on the ragstone ridge at Heath Farm and John's son Richard Mercer sold up the last family holding in East Malling and went for the safer option, grass and cattle in the shires.

When the Mercers sold Broadwater Lord Vestey bought it as a wedding present for his daughter. The marriage didn't take, but Broadwater became, before the word had been coined, a part of agrobusiness. Vesteys is the biggest private company in the land, a food combine with interests in Argentine beef ranches, the British butchery chain of Dewhursts, and a few farms of which Broadwater was the first.

They put Fred Stanley in as manager in the early 1960s. Stanley is the new kind of farm boss. He is a manager, not a farmer. He is a Wye College-trained agriculturist but he had no previous experience of hops and fruit. What he has is a deep strain of pragmatism. He watched the ancient rituals as hops were planted, with a man on stilts stringing up the poles. He knew that under the land was a mains system supplying stand-pipes and armour-plated hoses capable of withstanding pressures of 800 lb a square inch as they sprayed 300, 400, 500 gallons an acre of pesticide on the apples and pears and cherries and hops, and it took a dozen men to do the work. He watched the ritual of hop picking, as the East Enders swarmed down from London to live in the little brick hoppers' shacks and the gipsies knocked on the front door looking for work and the bines were cut down and the women and children stripped them by hand into bins and were paid by the bushel. And Fred Stanley watched the mystique of hop drying as the head drier reached into the kiln with a long ladle and scooped out a sample and rubbed it between thumb and forefinger and sniffed it like a rare and beautiful spice, and pronounced it ready without giving a reason, or silently shut the door of the kiln and bolted it for another half-hour. And the drier would order the boy to stoke up the furnace beneath the drying floor with more coke and tell him to be sure the little sulphur pan was burning so that the hops retained the delicate green that buyers liked. Fred Stanley watched all this, and he talked to the head drier and to his farm hands. And then he presided over his own agricultural revolution.

The immutable fact of life on the farm is the landscape. Broadwater is contained in a horseshoe curve of land rising to the north, south, and west. Water runs off the western incline and forms a stream and pond at Broadwater, then burrows underground to the source of the mill stream at Well Street (a corruption of the Old English *cwylla*, spring, like the Ewells dotted around the country). Broadwater is surrounded by the loam of the hundred-foot-thick Hythe beds, and its centre stands on a seam of head brick earth: perfect, as it happens, for fruit and hops; but brick making was a local industry too, and Charles Mercer turned Broadwater into the mansion it is today by building on to the Tudor ragstone and timber core with bricks from the Wells brothers on the Heath — a nice example of man making nature work for him to the full. Today the Wellses' brick pits are gentle declivities flourishing with lawns and flower beds and children on swings and centrally heated bungalows.

Broadwater has always been good farming land. The lanes round about are deeply cut into the loam so that the surfaces first tar-macadamed by the district council in Charles Mercer's time are ten and fifteen feet below the field levels: they speak of centuries of farm traffic. From the high ground to the south of the farm buildings you can see across to the tower of Malling Abbey in a belt of trees splashing deep green against the pale downs beyond. Broadwater itself has crept across the boundary of West Malling as far as Gundulf's other tower, St Leonard's, a mile south-west, and up to Lavender Road where a hawthorn hedge seven hundred years old interspersed with oak and alder and bramble and field maple and birch and ivy once enclosed Abbey lands.

Enclosure was and is the rule. Other counties went through the Middle Ages with open fields, then suffered enclosure, and have come into the late twentieth century spread out again into prairies. Kent, for hard economic reasons, has broadly speaking remained the same as always. Abraham Walter, gentleman, was the tenant of a small Twisden farm opposite the Bull in Larkfield. He surveyed for the second baronet all the Twisden holdings, and though Broadwater has grown, the core — which was the entire farm when Walter was at work — is today as it was then in 1682, the same field pattern, the very names the same. Now the fields are numbered, but Bob Fisher, Fred Stanley's oldest hand, still talks of Long Field and Water Down and Watery Down Bottom and Springett Hill Field and House Yards and Hemplott and Dickly and Lovelocks, the names Abraham Walter inscribed on his map. Walter did not specify crops, only the timber elms, and there is not much to go on except supposition and circumstantial evidence. When Robert Whittle, who you might think from the terms of his will was the village butcher but was actually the village parson, drew up his will in 1697, he bequeathed 'unto my loving sister Esther Gostling the wife of William Gostling tallow chandler all those my messuage, barns, stable, and slaughter house yards & gardens & that peece of land beyond the churchyard planted with hopps . . .'.

Hops had first been intensively cultivated by Flemish immigrants to Kent in the previous century; the Flemish, too, introduced market gardening. Kent was the perfect county. It had what Lord Ernle called 'the monopoly of proximity' to London; and London was even more pre-eminent in terms of comparative size and trading importance in the late sixteenth and early seventeenth centuries than it is now. In 1650 London's docks unloaded 989 shipments of corn: 527 of them from Kent alone. Daniel Defoe described Maidstone and its countryside a couple of decades after Abraham Walter's map and summed up in two short paragraphs of his *A Tour Through England and Wales* the economic pressures

and the geography that still shape Fred Stanley's farming strategy today.
Maidstone, Defoe wrote,

is a considerable town, very populous and the inhabitants generally
wealthy: 'tis the county town, and the river Medway is navigable to it
by large hoys, of fifty to sixty tuns burthen, the tide flowing quite up
to the town; round this town are the largest cherry orchards, and the
most of them that are in any part of England; and the gross of the
quantity of cherries, and the best of them which supply the whole city
of London come from hence, and are therefore call'd Kentish cherries.

Here likewise, and in the country adjacent, are great quantities of
hops planted, and this is call'd the Mother of Hop Grounds in England:
being the first place in England where hops were planted in any
quantity, and long before any were planted at Canterbury, tho' that
be now supposed to be the chief place in England, as shall be observ'd
in its place: These were the hops, I suppose, which were planted at the
beginning of the Reformation, and which gave occasion to that old
distich:

> Hops, Reformation, bays, and beer,
> Came into England all in a year.

Maidstone, Aylesford, Mill Hall, New Hythe, were the inland ports
for these fifty- and sixty-ton hoys, and even when the railway came in
1856 it followed the line of the Medway with stations at those wharves.
Not until 1874 could Broadwater load produce on a train bound for
London rather than the port of Rochester. Recorded from the time of
Edward III, but probably working there since the Roman occupation,
the Medway ships fed the maw of London. Timber went to Rochester
from New Hythe, fuller's earth to Colchester and the smaller ports of
East Anglia, fruit, corn, faggots to London and, since London has always
built with ragstone, ragstone too. The risks of shipping were spread right
through the parish, shared by farmers, maltsters, tailors, cordwainers.

And then there were the men who made their living directly from the
wharves at New Hythe: John Halle of 'Newheth' in the time of Edward
III, Robert Ewen, alias Robard Hewan, master of the *Thomas* of New-
hythe in 1481, John undyr Wode, master of the *Mare Mallyng* and
William Spryng, master of the *Barbara* of Maliun in 1478; Richard
Clements, 'Maryner of newe hithe in the pisshe of Estmalling' in 1518;
Thomas Gybson 'of East Mallyng in the countye of Kent marryner' in
1563; James Maylim of Newhide, shipwright, 1597, James Maylim, hoy-

man, 1653, and James Maylim, waterman, of East Malling, 1684; John Taylor, cordwainer of Newhide, 1680; John Shepherd, hoyman of Newhith, 1695; William Falsbury, sailmaker, 1698; Thomas Payn, aged thirteen 'or thereabouts', a poor child of East Malling, apprenticed to Francis Aldridge, hoyman of Snodland, 1775.

Broadwater used New Hythe wharf to take deliveries of coke for the boilers in the oasts, even though Charles Miles, the tenant farmer in the first half of the nineteenth century, only had ten acres of hops: when Charles Mercer grubbed the last five acres in Springett Hill Field in 1912, the oral tradition on the farm was that they were the last of Charles Miles's ten acres and had been there for a hundred years. Nothing is likely to last that long ever again. Hops with fresh qualities are bred and grown, discarded and grubbed; apple trees that grow only to the height of a man and yield heavily have displaced the big old trees that lasted so long but were less convenient and had a lower yield. And the machine has all but taken over.

Bob Fisher has worked at Broadwater since he was fourteen, in 1923, so he has seen most of the changes. He was born near Heath Farm in 1909. At two and a half he moved with his mother and father and older brother by horse and cart to the cottage where he still lives above Long Field. His father was a horse man at Broadwater from the turn of the century. He would be up at five o'clock in the morning, spend from six until two with the horses, then move on to other jobs. At seven in the evening he would go home for a cup of char and then back to clean the horses out for the following day. Bob's older brother was the farm's last horse man. Bob himself began as an oast boy, sweeping up, putting oil in the lamps and cleaning the lamp glasses, cutting string for the pokes (the sacks which hold the green hops), humping the pokes upstairs, helping to spread the hops out in the kiln, making the tea, breaking the coal.

'See, it was all kind of manual work that time of day, you'd got to carry everything. Even the coal you'd got to wheel in with a wheelbarrow and break that all up, that sort of thing. It was all manual work that time of day. Now you see all you do is just light these burners and it's all automatic more or less.'

Since then Bob has done every job on the farm: running the gang of twelve men spraying the hops and fruit; cutting back the hop bine in early winter with knives improvised from the thin steel slats that used to do duty instead of bedsprings, plus a piece of old bicycle tyre as the handle; camping out under canvas with a gun for six weeks at a time in the cherry orchards to scare the birds off; cutting down the chestnut in Hoath Wood in winter to make fences and hop poles; looking after the horses.

There were fourteen horses when Bob worked for Charles Mercer. Most were used in ploughing and hoeing in the hop gardens, but following the wartime priority, there was more arable than Broadwater has today. Bob Fisher remembers the old self-binder, the early combine harvester that cut the corn and bound it into stooks: the all-in machine that threshed it as well was a later invention. Three horses pulled the self-binder, but even then their days were numbered. One of the fourteen horses on the farm was used as the van horse, for light work like picking up parcels from the railway station. Then one day Charles Mercer sold the horse and bought a Ford lorry. That was the beginning. The next thing was a tractor to pull the self-binder, and the next thing the steam engine, the sort they show in carnivals and agricultural shows.

'They used to plough the fields with them old steam engines one time o' day. They'd have a rope between two engines and one paid it out and the other took it in. Then when the plough got down to one end they'd turn it round and send it back the other way. A man would sit on it to guide it, but it din't want all that much guiding. Last one I saw on Broadwater was in this field just down here, Long Field. They used to work their way along the edges of the field. A long time before the war that was. Matter of fact, I think it was before Vesteys took it over, and they took it over in 1926.'

But horses lingered until the 1950s, and Bob was looking after them again in the war. 'I was exempt in the war. Had to do fire watching and had to join what they called the Home Guard. We used to have to do two nights a week up at the aerodrome on guard. And then we had to go to work next morning, never got no time off. We used to work two hours off and two hours on up there. Farm working was hard during the war.

'You had to be careful where you got to, see, all these here aeroplanes and that and you'd got horses to look after and you'd got bombs dropping. Depend on what sort of horse you'd got. If you'd got one a bit nervy you had to keep your wits about you. We hadn't got many like that, just one or two and you'd know which one it was and you'd got to really keep an eye on it. I didn't have a lot to do with horses. I don't know, I suppose I had three or four years with the horses altogether. Then I was took off that and put on the tractors.'

Machinery meant more than the end of horses. When Vesteys moved in, Bob Fisher was one of a staff of forty men at Broadwater. After the war there were twenty-five. Today Fred Stanley reckons to employ fifteen, 'and of those a couple are semi-retired. That leaves thirteen men and three of them are only twenty and one's just a school-leaver.' And although there are fewer hops now, there are more fruit trees. The difference is in simpler spraying techniques, different cultivation, more machines. When Fred Stanley tots up the inventory of hardware, it sounds like an ordnance depot:

'We've got in the region of 150 electric motors, running from fractional-horsepower motors for driving automatic valves in the cold store or an electric drill in the workshop up to 50-horsepower. We've got some 25s and 30s and 10s and 15s, that sort of thing. It's quite surprising. And then when one talks about pneumatic tyres, well, 12 tractors, that's 48, 24 of them enormous big ones, a lorry with 6, 2 Land Rovers, that's another 8, that's 62, 2 vans, that's 70, 4 spraying machines, each with a pair, another 8, 78; then we've got 14 trailers, some of them two-wheeled, some of them four, so we're probably talking about 36 tyres on the trailers, so that's 110 tyres already. You'd probably find that we have 120 pneumatic tyres at least, of varying sizes. And then of course there's quite a few things with solid tyres, like mowers.'

In 1966 Fred Stanley spent £10,000 — less a grant of £2,000 — on a hopping machine, and with that brought to an abrupt end a four-hundred-year-old agricultural tradition. From cutting the hops from the pole, to stripping them from leaves and stalk and collecting them in hop bins made of sacking to drying them and packing them in pockets the process remained much the same. There were minor variations. W. Weeks's hop press was one. Before that a farm hand trod the hops into the pockets, so that the eighteenth-century Kentish poet Christopher Smart warned the farmer in jingoistic Miltonic measure:

> When in the bag the hops the rustic treads,
> Let him wear heel-less sandals; nor presume
> Their fragrancy barefooted to defile:
> Such filthy ways for slaves in Malaga
> Leave we to practise . . .

Then there was a change in the way the hop bines were grown. Twine until after the war had been a farmer's luxury and the bines were trained straight up hop poles. Now rows of hop poles carry a chequerwork of overhead wire, and the bines are trained up twine tied to the wire above and moored to the ground with hooks like crude tent pegs.

But neither of these changes in themselves meant fewer hands at hopping time. And when George Orwell hiked out from London to pick hops on the Blest Farm in Wateringbury with the gipsies and East Enders (the Blests too are automated today), he couldn't have quarrelled with Smart's description:

> See! from the great metropolis they rush,
> Th' industrious vulgar. They, like prudent bees,
> In Kent's wide garden roam, expert to crop
> Th' flowery hop . . .

Above Broadwater in Well Street are the tiny hopper huts, in ruins already, brick built with corrugated tin roofs and a communal lavatory to each block of huts: hovels, some would say, but London families returned year after year and played hell if they couldn't have the same huts. Colleges at the ancient universities ran welfare services for the hoppers and the Red Cross manned dispensaries: philanthropists, who were then what sociologists are now, came, saw, and pondered over the intimate squalor but concluded that after all it was better than the normal slum life of Lambeth and the East End. The vicar worried about the morals, the hopper marriages that lasted a fortnight, the disturbingly pagan note to the drunken harvest celebrations, and if he couldn't entice the hoppers down to the church, well, he would jolly well hold a service for them in a marquee on waste ground near the huts (the boy Bob Fisher crept up with a small gang of friends and slackened the guy ropes so that the marquee collapsed in the middle of 'All Things Bright and Beautiful').

This seasonal labour force worked in gangs of a dozen, more or less, each gang under a regular farm hand acting as bin man. A farm hand freed the bine from its hop pole with a long rod and the labour gang stripped the fruit from the bine, collected it in a basket, and transferred the basketful to a hop bin made of sacking.

They earned according to whatever the tally was in that year: the tally was the number of bushels required for each shilling paid out. In Charles Mercer's time at Broadwater it could be anything between five and eight. In his son John's time at Heath Farm, the tally book for 1958 shows that the tally was one: one bushel picked, one shilling paid out.

That year picking went on from 3 September to 25 September, and in those twenty working days one really fast operator made a grand total of £56.19s. The norm was nearer £35. And now tractors and trailers, a conveyor belt, and a few students do the work.

On this particular bright September morning when Fred Stanley in his windcheater is supervising the hop-stripping, the tractors are out in Watery Down. Today's binman is in a crow's nest at the top of the tractor's hydraulic lift, cutting the bine from the overhead wire with a brush hook (which outside Kent is known as a sickle) so that it drops into the trailer. Every ten minutes a tractor with a fresh trailer-load of hops bounces across Broadwater Road to the main cluster of farm buildings — the house, the oast with its five white-cowled kilns, workshops, ancient barn, fruit packing plant, cold store, and, at the foot of the oast, the fifty-yard-long shed that houses the hop-stripping machine. The tractor noses in through a door in the north side of the shed and parks outside the south door with the trailer at rest in the shed under what looks like a giant's bicycle chain moving in an ellipse parallel to the floor. A girl in anorak and jeans climbs into the trailer and another student forks a tangle of hop bine up to her. She attaches it to one of the clips suspended from the chain, hacking with a brush hook at the worst of the tangle. The clip feeds the bine into the maw of what is basically a conveyor belt with teeth, the delicate hop cones are separated from bine and debris and leaves in three succeeding operations, and the leaves descend in a gentle green cascade along a chute and through the air on to a soft leaf drift in the farm yard.

All that's left now is the hop fruit and its aromatic odour. The hops tumble on to another conveyor belt studded with little steps that carry the hops up to the platform outside the oast's drying floor. A student bags the hops into pokes, secures the necks of the pokes, and wheels them on a trolley into the main floor of the oast, ready for the kilns. Fred Stanley, half a dozen students manning the hop-stripping machine, the tractors and the brush hooks have put an end to the special trains from London, the back-breaking labour, the gipsies camping on the Heath and in Well Street, the heavy boozing in the village pubs, the fornication in the fields and woods, the lightning strikes over the tally that nearly always collapsed for lack of organisation — Orwell had it that women and gipsies were too stupid to see the advantages of unions.

At any rate the gipsies have retreated from the farms. Maybe it was inevitable. The hop-stripping machine was the end of a long process. For three hundred years the gipsies moved from farm to farm and found employment through the seasons, hoeing and scything, harvesting peas and strawberries and cherries in summer, cabbages and Brussels sprouts in early winter, planting out cabbages and broccoli, running a caravan industry from the coppice woods making tree stakes, fence stakes, fence posts, gate posts, hop poles. They were strong, and could do back-breaking work, they were practised in agricultural lore and could do skilled work. Now they are relegated to their reservations, forced back into flibberty-gibbet trades: laying tarmac drives, breaking up old cars, dealing in scrap metal.

The survivors of the revolution have been what Fred Stanley calls his regular part-timers, about two dozen housewives, women like Mrs Fisher and others whose husbands work at the Research Station or in the mills. Mrs Fisher has been working at Broadwater ever since she married Bob in 1934 in St James's church. Bob remembers that the reception was at the working men's club in Ditton. 'And when we came home from the reception, you know what we came home in? A coal lorry.' Mrs Fisher says: 'Oh, we said, that'll bring us some luck. And we haven't had any luck since, have we?'

Mrs Fisher was in service until then at Loose, earning £4 a month. She started at Broadwater at 19s.4½d. The work was much as it is today: in spring and early summer training the hop bines and cutting and packing asparagus; after the holiday picking apples and pears, in winter pruning the trees and cutting suckers out of the Bramley trees. Fruit packing still has to be done, in crates, but grading is mechanised now. Fruit used to be packed in bushel baskets. Bob Fisher says: 'You'd have to kind of ring the apples into the basket, see, lie them round in rings. And if those were packed properly you could turn them upside down, you know, and they wouldn't fall out. If they were put in as they should be. They put blue paper all round the inside. When they got it full they used to put a piece of blue paper over the top and then straw and then pack it with two sticks, nut sticks, crosswise over the top. That's the way they used to pack, that time of day. Then they'd take them down to the station and send them up to Covent Garden. Cherries used to go in like half-bushel baskets. But they used to put a piece of blue paper around and then the straw on the cherries, blue piece of paper on the top, the grower's name and address on the paper faced upwards, just two sticks across. I don't think today you could do that, transporting fruit like that.'

Imports undercutting British prices, Algerian settlers in France subsidised to grow Golden Delicious apples, bigger conglomerates in brewing — change would have come anyway to the farming industry. Fat pay packets and the Costa Brava dimmed the appeal of the hopper huts. Richard Mercer might arrange for thirty casuals at hopping time, and only half would arrive. The cattle in Shropshire are more reliable. So the gale that blew down his new hop garden was, so to say, only the last blow.

Sentiment apart, does anyone really mind the changes? The villagers disliked the annual invasion. Machinery has ushered in bigger profits. Regular farm hands like Bob Fisher are better off, though with a minimum rate of not much more than £40 and a few pounds on top for craftsman qualifications, they are still way down at the bottom of the wages table.

'I used to fetch the women from Snodland up here for the black currant picking,' Bob Fisher says: 'I was talking one day and they said Well I don't see what you've got to grumble about because you get everything supplied from the farm, potatoes and green stuff and fruit and all that sort of thing. Oo's told you a tale like that? I said. I said, Well, you swop over, I said, you have what I get next week and I'll take your wages.'

At Snodland or New Hythe a labourer might pick up a craft wage for his skill with a dumper or a tractor. At Broadwater any given farm hand might know about planting and pruning, barley and asparagus and black currants, apples and pears, driving a tractor, training the hop bines. He may know the uses of a dozen different sprays and which need to be handled with protective clothing. He clear ditches and drains and repairs brickwork. And there's a genius, the others say, who looks after the farm machinery.

One farmer, not Fred Stanley, described farm workers to me as the salt of the earth. It's a phrase with a fine old paternalistic ring to it, and it would cause a walkout in most heavy industries. And yet it is true. Job satisfaction is an indeterminable commodity. Or is it just that the nature of the work makes an effective union impossible to organise? 'After you've been used to going, going, going,' Bob Fisher says, 'you come home, you sit down, like on a wet day, you can't keep still. The other day I went to work, it'd been snowing, the manager and his wife said I'm surprised at you turning up, thought you'd have stayed away. I said I'd have thought you'd knowed better. I don't mind the life really. We have the ups and downs, soon forget about it.'

For all their comparative poverty, most farm hands own a car and run it to work, even if it is only half a mile away. Bob Fisher and his wife don't, but their warmly furnished cottage has wall-to-wall carpet, colour television, and a record deck with stereo speakers. Bob brings on the seedlings for the kitchen garden in his greenhouse (there's a small lean-to conservatory as well) and out front he has the neatest flower beds in his end of Well Street.

There is no doubt that change has been for the better. Merrie Englande hardly existed, and from the Napoleonic Wars through the hungry 1840s the English land labourer was worse off than any in Europe. John Larking's son, Lambert Larking, parson and scholar, was born at Clare House in 1797 and lived through these times as vicar of Ryarsh near by. He produced a famous facsimile annotated edition of the Kent pages of the Domesday Book and in his commentary he felt moved to compare the labourer's lot with the slave's in Edward the Confessor's Kent:

> The experience of nearly half a century in watching over the privations and hardships and sufferings of this class, enables me to confirm the assertion. . . . The agricultural labourer is, to all intents and purposes, a slave; though happily, ignorant of his bondage. The very Poor Laws of which we make our national boast, are often converted into engines to rivet his fetters.

What of the other sorts of change? Kent is unimaginable without hops, yet for Fred Stanley and other growers the future is a throw of the dice. Hops are at the mercy of international market forces, lack of EEC co-ordination, pressure from the brewers, an unsentimental band of brothers whose attempt to force pressurised, chemicalised, carbonised beer down the throats of all beer drinkers foundered on a successful customers' revolt, but who still believe above all in tidy accounts and beer that stays drinkable for ever.

For the grower, part of the problem is the sheer range of choice. There are hops called Fuggles and there are hops called Goldings; there are Wye Target and Wye Saxon and Brambling Cross and Early Bird and Janus and Bullion. Bullion is the sort the tractors are bringing to the hop-stripping machine from Watery Down: it isn't much use for the lighter beers, but for Guinness it is perfect (Broadwater has been supplying 'Messrs A. Guinness of Dublin' since 1910). When Fred Stanley came to Broadwater he had seven acres of Early Birds, but they were susceptible to verticilium wilt, the ground-borne virus that all hop growers dread. He heard that Janus was the hop of the future, so the plan was to replace Early Bird with Janus.

'Well, these hops are bred at Wye. They have growers' trials. Before they are generally distributed they have brewers' trials by the Institute of Brewing, and the brewers themselves say yes, this is the hop we want, and the growers plant them up. And within five years the brewers say, Sorry old boy, we don't want that one. And you're back to square one.'

The other aspect of the problem is summed up by Bob Fisher. Remarking on the decreased acreage of Broadwater's hop gardens, he observes laconically: 'There's more chemicals, like, put into the beer today.'

In fact, before the First World War Professor Salmon at Wye College quietly published a finding that he had stumbled upon in his laboratory. The useful component of the hop, he announced, was its alpha acid. His finding lay fallow until the 1960s, when the Germans and Americans started cooking up hop extracts in the laboratory which were concentrations of alpha acids: a kind of molasses with a practically indefinite shelf life. Hop powder and pelleted hops followed in short order and the big brewers sat up and rubbed their hands. My God, they said, this means continuous brewing instead of batch brewing; and powders and pills don't clog up pipes and valves and filters the way the whole hop does.

'Well,' Fred Stanley says, 'the big brewers decided around 1970 that it was the high alphas they wanted and mainly because it was very much more attractive for them to buy a hop with an alpha of 9 per cent than a hop with an alpha of 4.5 per cent. And of course they only wanted half as much hop. And that is what has happened and is happening. And again Wye have come up trumps by breeding hops with high alpha content, and most of us over the last three or four years have been gradually propagating and restructuring our hop gardens by planting these wilt-resistant high-alpha hops. The net result is that the hop acreage must inevitably shrink even further.'

So Fred Stanley will grow Wye Target and Wye Saxon and he will reduce his acreage to 20 from the current 28. Except, and there always is an except, at the last turn of the merry-go-round he was about to grub up his outmoded Whitbread Golden Variety when there was a sudden demand for it, maybe because there was a shortfall somewhere else in the market. Who knows? So, like other growers, Fred Stanley is hanging on, balancing EEC support grants against the knowledge that in a year when British hops were selling at about £80 a dried hundredweight, the Germans, organised on a peasant basis with small acreages and small labour costs, overproduced and were offloading on to the complaisant European market at £20 a hundredweight.

Whatever his decision, which could be to get out of it altogether, it will be taken on a purely practical basis. As a manager, Fred Stanley has no financial stake in the outcome. He lives in the splendour of a farmhouse built for more spacious times, with a kitchen big enough to feed an army and a sitting room like the *Mauretania*'s saloon. Otherwise, he is like any other company representative. He drives a small family car, is given expense-account lunches in Maidstone by fertiliser and herbicide company reps, is a member of the Lions, where he can meet other businessmen and trade experiences with them. His work is determined by factors that have not changed since man stopped being a hunter, but to the extent that he can conquer the dictates of nature with a slide rule he will do it. And he will do it without compunction or sentiment. He will talk of varieties of eating apple, Worcester, Golden Delicious, Katya, Crispin (which is the Japanese Mutsu), Idle Red (which is American), Blenheim, Martha Turner, and Suntan, a new apple about to be launched on the market after development at East Malling Research Station. And then he comes to Britain's pride, Cox's Orange Pippin. Cox's? he says. 'I think probably Cox's, if you were a retired wing commander and you had five acres adjacent to your house, would be a reasonable thing.' Well yes, he says; without a doubt Cox is the best eating apple there is, unbeatable flavour, fetches the highest price per box. But then he recalls the day he dismayed his assistant with his heretical views, so he sat down and drew up a list of pros and cons. Pro: flavour and price. 'But when I started jotting down my notes on the con side, I ran out of paper.'

Just for starters, it seems that its average cropping is under a puny 250 boxes an acre, well under. It is susceptible, seemingly, to every pest, disease, and marginal soil deficiency in the business. It needs the most expensive spray programme the genius of man can devise to produce what Fred Stanley would grudgingly admit as a decent leaf or a decent quality fruit. Finally, crushingly, Fred Stanley says: 'I have heard of a farm not two miles from where we are sitting at this moment, of a five-year Golden Delicious orchard which produced a thousand bushels an acre in its fifth year. Now I don't know of *any* Cox orchard which has *ever* produced a thousand bushels an acre.'

When he finally decides to grub these orchards, he will not be alone, and he will sleep a lot easier knowing he has no Cox's. Or plums. Or cherries. Or strawberries. Ah, yes: strawberries. 'I mean, what the hell do you do with a big acreage on, sort of, the Whit weekend? You know they've got to be picked, they're not going to stop ripening because it's the Whit weekend. And what do you do with Friday's strawberries, because there's not a market worth sending fruit to open on Saturday and on Sunday it's closed, Monday it's closed. And in Jubilee year, Tuesday it was closed as well. If it gets really hot the strawberries fry in the sun and if it gets wet they rot.

'I don't know why we grow things at all.'

# 5 The automated ecological time bomb

**Kent, sir — everybody knows Kent — apples, cherries, hops, and women.**   Dickens, Pickwick Papers

*Gig Hill Farm from Walter's maps of the Twisden Estate*

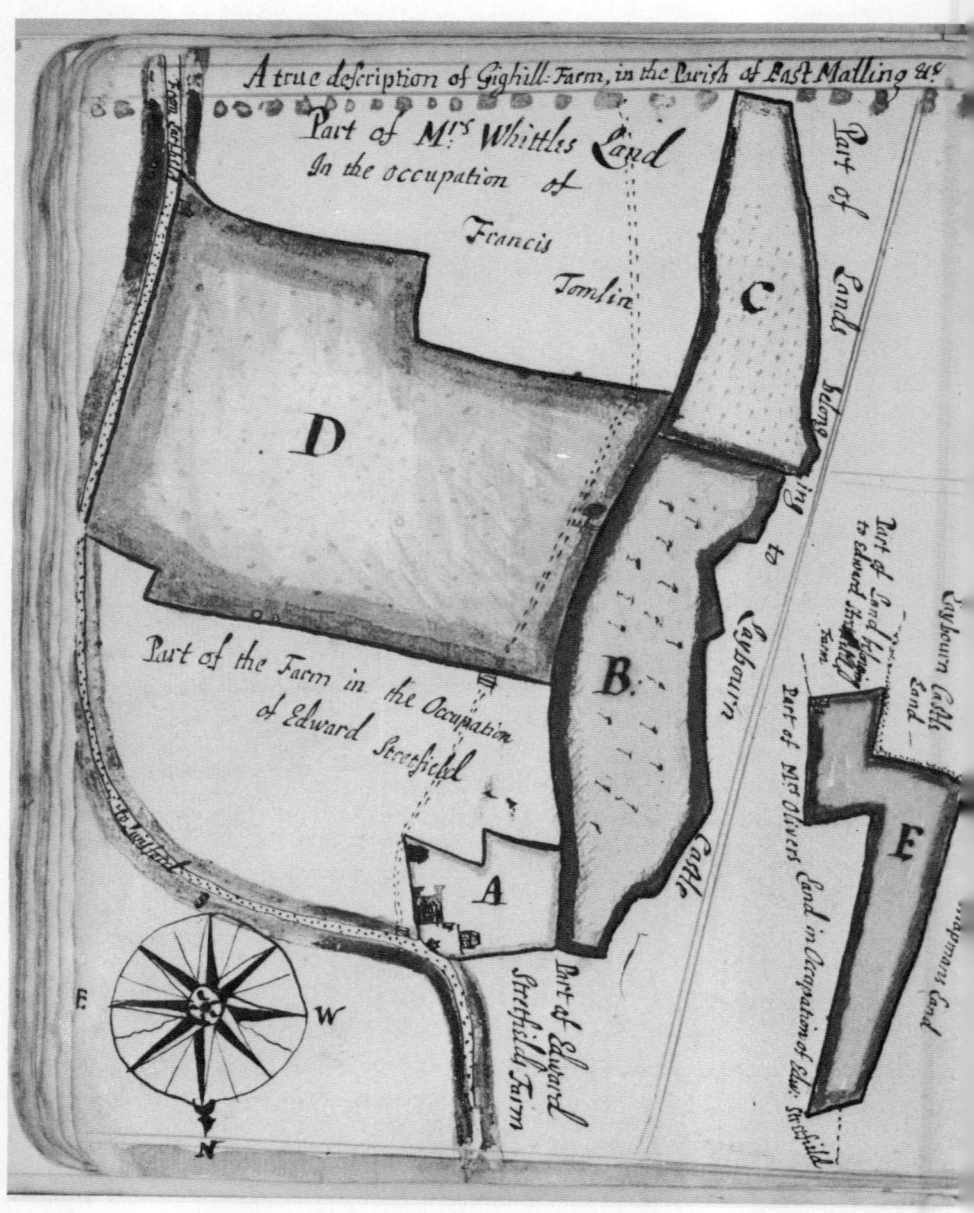

ONE OF THE windows in Dr Rutherford's department at East Malling Research Station looks across the village's ancient common field, Great East, at the church of St James. A quarter of a mile separates Dr Rutherford's offices from the church; a quarter of a mile and a thousand years. Dr Rutherford tends the computer brain of the Research Station. And the Research Station exists to give the Fred Stanleys of England reasons for growing things.

| Gig=hill Farm, | Acres | R | Perches |
|---|---|---|---|
| A: Gighill & Yard house & Barn — | 1 | 0 | 18 |
| B: The Alders ——— | 5 | 0 | 09 |
| C: The Hopground —— | 2 | 3 | 36 |
| D: Lunsford Broomes —— | 12 | 2 | 17 |
| E: Crooked Mead — | 2 | 0 | 27 |
| The Sum of Acres  - - - - | 23 | 3 | 27 |

Dr Rutherford is an athletic-looking, grey-haired, blue-eyed Irish en-
thusiast who works from a bare little office, linoleum-floored, a yearly
job planner on one wall, a bookcase filled with volumes of the *Journal of
the Royal Statistical Society*, a sparsely covered notice board decorated with
a large round lapel badge bearing the inconsequential slogan, 'Dijkstra
gives me microphobia.' He is a postwar agriculturist who moved into
statistics in 1954 when, short of counting beads, a small hand-cranked
machine was about the only mechanical aid to calculation. In those days
a statistician might normally hope to solve something of the order of six
simultaneous equations. Dr Rutherford once solved fourteen; it took him
three weeks. Now, through a computer method called batch processing,
man-plus-machine might expect as a normal task to solve two hundred
or so simultaneous equations. 'We're far more inclined to solve everything you can think of now,' Dr Rutherford says. 'And a good many
things you can't think of.'

One of the things he would sooner not think of is how to work out in
spring what the year's apple harvest will be like. An impossible task,
since there are imponderables like a good gust of wind or two which no
computer yet invented can predict; but a task which Dr Rutherford is
constantly being asked to tackle. He is, he says, on a hiding to nothing.

Dr Rutherford's department of statistics processes vast quantities of
information about the station's research work. It carries out three main
operations. It has a tin box, the size of a tall man, that is all electronic brain.
This is linked to an apple grader: the sort farms use for sorting and packing apples according to size but in a souped-up version that registers not
just size and weight, but colour and something else called its russet
quality, which sounds like colour but is actually texture of skin. This
grading machine incorporates one of those inventions which, like the
wheel, looks ultra-simple once it is there but is, in the immortal words of
President Nixon, a giant step forward for man. Research man at least.
The grader is a modified conveyor belt: at the point where colour and
russet quality is tested, it has two rubber belts half an inch or so apart
running at different speeds so that the apple is constantly turning at a
constantly varying tangent like a tiny Cox's planet, and the researcher
sees the whole of the surface of each apple as it slowly spins before him
instead of the normal 60 per cent.

The whole world of the computer linked to the apple grader is the
colour, weight, and skin quality of apples. The other two statistics department operations are, roughly speaking, a question-and-answer teleprinter link to a central computer at Rothamstead Experimental Station

in Hertfordshire and a fast system for handling batches of jobs, often whole research programmes. Not that the first system (in the computer man's jargon, interactive) is exactly slow. Any toiler in the orchard at East Malling Research Station can wander up and feed requests for information to Rothamstead and receive his answers from the computer at ten characters a second: about the speed at which BBC-TV's *Grandstand* receives its football results. But the batch system links to Rothamstead through a Honeywell tin box called a 725G Job Entry Terminal at the sensational speed of 3,000 characters a second: whole tapes swallowed and spat out while you blink. A pause of a minute or two and the printout from Rothamstead follows much faster than the eye can trace.

Rothamstead is the agriculturist's computer capital. A diagram showing research centres linked to Rothamstead looks like an ancient map of the military outposts of the empire linked to Rome. All over England (plus the Unit of Statistics at Edinburgh University) agricultural research centres are linked to Rothamstead. Not all of them: a couple of dozen all told. Like the fruit research station at Long Ashton, near Bristol; Langford Meat Research Station, again near Bristol; the Glasshouse Crops Research Institute at Littlehampton and the Grassland Research Institute near Maidenhead; the Wheat Research Institute, near Oxford; the National Vegetable Research Station, near Stratford-upon-Avon; the National Institute for Research in Dairying, near Reading; the Food Research Station at Norwich; the Plant Breeding Institute and the Institute of Animal Physiology, both near Cambridge; the Letcombe Laboratory near Wantage (where Dr Rutherford himself once worked on the level of strontium 90 deposited in our food by nuclear bomb explosions); the Agricultural Research Council in Great Portland Street, London, which funds the biggest fruit research station in the world, at East Malling.

If an American fruit grower thinks of England at all, he thinks about East Malling. So does a Russian, a Nepalese, a Japanese. Nina Bassuk from New York had heard of East Malling (where she works now on plant propagation) before she had heard of Kent. And the reason is apple root stock, which is to apple growing what the American vine root stock is to wine production. The root stock that has transformed the world's approach to the art and science of apple production was developed at East Malling Fruit Research Station. 'The Research' has 600 acres of prime land. And every rod, pole, and perch on it has been mapped and photographed and re-mapped and re-photographed from observation aircraft and the results of all these separate studies superimposed in the records branch run by Sheila Pryor within Dr Rutherford's department.

Sheila Pryor is a mild, donnish-looking woman (the atmosphere in the Research Station is like a university's and doctors are as thick on the ground as in a Central European capital) whose interest in the history of the Research Station orchards and hop gardens is anything but altruistic: every scientist in the station needs to know the past use of the land and its relevance to his experiments (there are 100 graduate researchers on a staff of 400, 180 scientific assistants, plus farm workers, cooks, clerical staff, cleaners, brickies, plumbers, and carpenters).

The traceable land use goes back to the Roman occupation. From time to time workmen with their spades turn up in Millens field ceramic tesserae from the first-century Roman villa. Half a mile to the north archaeologists working on the Tudor foundations of Bradbourne itself have discovered the first signs of an original Roman building, and another half-mile north, over the London Road in Larkfield, is a Roman burial ground. And one of Sheila Pryor's aerial photographs shows the distinct mark of a long, straight road in Bradbourne Park parallel to the modern London Road: the military road, probably, first mentioned in a ninth-century document. So the Romans or the Romano-British farmed here. Some authorities suppose that they adopted the original Celtic system of enclosed fields and that this survived more or less intact in Kent while most other English villages divided their arable land into strip fields (Parliamentary Enclosure in Kent affected no single arable field, only common and waste land). The exception to the rule in East Malling was Est Field, as the Abbess knew it in 1410, which was divided among villagers and survived as an open three-strip field until the eighteenth century. Today, it's the field known as Great East, between Dr Rutherford and the church.

Sheila Pryor's documents and a study made by two senior scientists record this; and where there was a rookery and what the field consisted of when the trees fell before the axe; where there was a row of elm; how the footpath to Maidstone was widened, the part of the park that became a hop garden when the Twisdens let it out as farm land; the obliteration of field boundaries and the creation of others. In 1959 the Research Station acquired land called Ditton Rough, which restored to Bradbourne a field which had first been mentioned in 1602 by John Manningham. He is one of the better-known diarists of the period, partly because he recorded his impressions of an early performance of *Twelfth Night*, partly for his lively account of London life in general and court life in particular. Political historians turn to him for his account of Queen

Elizabeth's death, relayed to him by his friend the Queen's chaplain: 'This morning about three at clocke, hir Majestie departed this lyfe, mildly like a lambe, easily like a ripe apple from the tree,' John Manningham wrote. The countryside simile came easily: Manningham was a frequent visitor to his kinsman Richard Manningham at Bradbourne, and on 18 April 1602 he recorded: 'My cosen concluded with William Tunbridge of Ditton to give him £115 for a leas of Ditton ruffe for 25 years.'

The Research Station would have preferred John Manningham to have said what his cousin proposed doing with the field, but he didn't. Whatever it was — arable, pasture, or fruit — it was certainly not the same use as it is now put to by the Research Station. The Ordnance Survey geological map shows that Ditton Rough stands, like most of Bradbourne's lands, on the ragstone Hythe beds. There are seams of fuller's earth, some alluvial soil around the mill stream bed as it passes through Bradbourne, areas of sand on the Folkestone beds, and areas of rich brick earth which blew as dust on to the land towards the end of the Ice Age and settled in drifts; but mainly it is the loam of the Hythe beds. One reason why the Research Station alighted on East Malling in 1913 and bought its first field for a shilling was the quality of the soil, deep, well-drained, and medium-textured: uniform in large stretches, but outside the uniformity a wide variety. And there's the rub.

For the varieties of soil are vital to experiment, but in the variety lurk unknown hazards. Which is why the Research Station boffins crawl over the land so carefully before they plant a single seed or root or cutting. Even after they had analysed the soil of Great East in every conceivable way, things happened that cannot be accounted for. Like the great lime chlorosis mystery: an inexplicable and severe affliction in apple trees in a field south of Ditton Rough. Finally researchers turned up a map of the field of 1772 and found clearly marked the site of a lime kiln which, as the researchers sheepishly noted, explained the name of the plot, Kiln Field.

So the scientists like to know the history of their fields, down to the minutest particular. For Ditton Rough there was not much history. But then the geologists made trial borings at fifty-yard intervals. And within the known pattern of the soil and rock beneath, they made subdivisions according to the texture and depth: Barming series, Langley series, Wierton series — even a little tribute to their sponsor: Twisden series. And within these subdivisions further subdivisions, until at last the geologist in charge pronounced Ditton Rough excellent soil for setting out experiments. So on this featureless area of soil is a small orchard, a nursery, rows of gooseberry bushes, and on the little patch of brick earth a minute hop garden.

That isn't a bad cameo of the Research Station's work. The Bradbourne estate is nothing more nor less than a large farm turned open-air laboratory. Everything is fenced in. Across the top of the gate into Ditton Rough are several strands of barbed wire. Unlike the average fruit farmer, the Research Station cannot afford to lose its windfalls, and a few apples stripped from a tree by trespassers could wreck a year's project for a researcher.

Recently a rash of crested ties and scarves among the staff proclaimed that the station had won a Queen's Award for technology for its work on disease-resistant hops. The station doesn't develop new kinds of hop, mark you: anything Wye College can develop, says Dr Rutherford, we can give verticilium wilt. Which is one way of explaining how work is divided between the two establishments (Wye won an award too).

East Malling modestly reckoned its work was worth a million pounds sterling a year to the hop growers. Not that the station likes to think simply in vulgar terms of how much the cash register rings up, but after all the taxpayer does shell out around £1.8 millions a year not counting capital costs — though not, thank you very much, through the Government. The Agricultural Research Council allots it from its own budget of £50 millions, so East Malling keeps its freedom to carry out, well, not quite pure research, but pretty fundamental stuff.

Like micropropagation. That is still in the test tube but basically it is a way of producing, say, 10,000 apple tree shoots from one cutting. When they can find a way of getting as many as a million root stocks from one plant — it's been done with things like orchids, but never with woody plants — that will be a real breakthrough. And they will.

Then there is the work on storing fruit. Standing apart from the rest of the laboratories is a strange brick building with a massive high pitched roof, as though a suburban bungalow had been adapted as a ship's drydock. Which in a sense it has: it was built so that East Malling's scientists could simulate conditions in a shipload of apples coming to Britain from the Cape or Australia. Suddenly the station's work on storage is even more important to Britain. The OPEC-dictated rise in oil prices has made transport from the southern hemisphere uneconomic, and the pride of Britain's orchards, Cox's Orange Pippin, keeps notoriously badly, as Fred Stanley gloomily argues at Broadwater Farm. But the

Research Station has pioneered keeping it until May — three months longer than previously — and now, by adapting the breathalyser test, they have made it feasible for Cox's to appear in greengrocers' shops in June; the new test detects increasing alcohol in the fruit, which is a sign that it is breaking down, and that is remedied by feeding more oxygen into the store.

Next, what to do about cherries? Around Faversham some cherries are still grown, but of the sight Celia Fiennes saw, 'from Rochester that night I went to Gravesend which is all by the side of Cherry grounds that are of severall acres of ground and runs quite down to the Thames', nothing. And in East Malling, nothing. Not a single acre. The only cherry tree near Broadwater is in Fred Stanley's assistant's garden, and the birds eat the cherries.

Fred Stanley gave up growing them years ago. The trees were too big and women pickers haven't the head for heights (so the Research Station has developed small trees). At the first hint of frost, cherry blossom is blighted (so East Malling is developing a hormone spray which safe-guards the growth of fruit even if frost hits the blossom). Finally, clinch-ingly, orchards planted after the war suffered from a bacterial canker which drastically reduced yield. Old farmers used to say you must plant stone after pip, pip after stone. But cherries grow best on brick earth, and if you are to alternate them with apple trees, that means growing them alternately on inferior soil. So East Malling is working on a resistant root stock. If East Malling could pull that off, it might, just, restore the cherry to favour with the big fruit growers. Money says it will, argues the director of the Research Station, Professor A. F. Posnette.

Then there is the plum pox problem. The fruit could be wiped out entirely in Britain, so the Research Station has a crash programme. The story begins in wartime Yugoslavia, where German soldiers so liked what they saw of the local plum, big, purple, succulent (and infected with plum pox), that they took it home to plant. The plum pox aphid swept down the Rhine Valley, leapt the Channel, and now if it becomes en-demic and infects the wild plum in the hedgerow, the fight will be lost. The only way until now of discovering plum pox in time involved a test with a time-lag of six weeks between test and results; and if the test was made in August there could be no results before the next spring. The test East Malling is developing gets instantaneous results: take the juice of several leaves, mix it with an anti-serum, and if it turns yellow you've got the pox.

It isn't a bad record of service to fruit-growing man. To be director of

East Malling Research Station is to be very nearly at the top of the tree. Departing directors have their portraits painted in oils and hung in the Bradbourne board room; more than likely they are knighted. But all the fruits of success could turn to ashes in Professor Posnette's mouth. The Research Station is sitting on an ecological time bomb, and he knows it.

East Malling's scientists pioneered modern pesticides and herbicides in fruit growing. The apple trees of every major fruit grower and a lot of the others grow in rows along neat alleys stripped by herbicides of all weeds. Grass and clover keep weeds down, but you have to compensate with massive doses of nitrogen to replace for the trees what the grass and clover take. Hoeing keeps the weeds down, but it damages the tree roots. So until something better comes along herbicides will stay. But pesticides used in massive, frequent, and regular spraying programmes are another matter; pesticides have upset the balance of nature. The red spider mite grows resistant to sprays as fast and faster than new ones can be developed, and meanwhile the sprays kill the insects that eat the vermin! As Professor Posnette puts it: 'The major thrust in our work is now towards the natural predator.' In other words, more ladybirds, not less, is the cry today.

So the boffins have their hands full, and they need their statistics department and they need their teleprinter link to the mechanical memory at Rothamstead. But the Honeywell 725G Job Entry Terminal? Why that sort of speed within what would now be called the parameters of a diurnal, seasonal rhythm, the budding, the blossoming, the fruiting, the harvesting?

Well, Dr Rutherford says, falling back on the not-quite-outdated human brain to make a series of rough calculations, there are 20,000 to 30,000 trees on the Research Station. Most of them will be put under observation five times a year. Each tree in a decent year will have, say, 100 apples. There are four colour categories for each apple and four russet categories. There is a weight category which, with the cross-referencing of colour and russet qualities (four multiplied by four), makes sixteen categories. Further information: how many apples are in the top categories. How different treatment affects similar apples, and how the particular plot affects them. The treatment of *each* apple produces 10 to 12 digits of information: that's 12,000 digits per plot. So a medium-size experiment of 70 plots of 60 or 70 trees will generate between 2 and 3 million characters.

Then there will be experiments on the form of the leaves, measurements of the girths of the trees, the weight of the prunings and the weight of the new extension growth left on the trees over winter. There might be a chemical analysis of some of the apples to relate to the treatment; an analysis of the effect of different periods of storage; of the variability of the crop yield related to the climate.

So it isn't smaller machine capacity they are looking for in the statistics department, but greater.

# 6 Recycling the past

**...the mill is set agoing by the water and at the same tyme it pounded the raggs to morter for the paper, and it beate oatmeale and hemp and ground bread together that is at the same tyme.**
The Journeys of Celia Fiennes (Kent, 1697)

*Abraham Walter's map showing John Tomlin's land by the springhead*

SINCE JOHN TOMLIN made paper on the mill stream in the 1680s, the technology has not changed much in basic principles. And the same mill pond still supplies water to Reed International. The difference is that Tomlin's paper was handmade; Reed International have thirteen machines each a hundred yards long in mills big enough to play football in. Reed International's five hundred acres sprawl across three parishes and obliterate boundaries. To distinguish it from other Reed Inter-

national operations, they call it Reed Aylesford, though most of it is in Ditton and the main gates and the administration buildings are in East Malling. It is the biggest paper mill in Europe. There are mills which make more newsprint, or more paper board, or more corrugated paper; and Reed Aylesford make no writing paper at all. But no mill in Europe turns out a greater combined quantity of greaseproof paper, blotting paper, electrical conductivity paper, white newsprint, coloured newsprint, bags, cement sacks, potato sacks, envelopes, paper for Pan books and for Corgi books, toilet rolls, serviette papers, Tate & Lyle sugar bags, or fluting (the middle crinkly bit in layered cardboard boxes). Reed say they make 400,000 tonnes of paper a year: that's EEC newspeak for about the same number of English tons.

Making paper is expensive. And making mistakes is very expensive. When there is a full order book, a shutdown for mechanical failure on the No. 6 board machine could cost Reed International £700 an hour, getting on for ten times what the average worker takes home in a week. When Reg Spice, the chief paper maker, started work in the early 1950s at Reed, the firm used to shut down once a year, on Christmas Day. It now reckons that sort of sentiment is folly. So it keeps going 24 hours a day, 365 days a year, employing 6,000 men, generating 54 megawatts of electricity — enough to keep a town the size of Brighton going — and still taking 17 or 18 megawatts off the grid as well.

If you can stand the hours, the life could be worse. Reed works a four-shift system. One man works from six in the morning until two, the next from two until ten, the next from ten until six, and the fourth man is on a rest day. That means each worker does seven days then has three days off, seven on, three off, four weeks holiday, eight bank holidays: not so good if your wife is at work, good if you've got children around the house, not so good when they are at school age, good when they have grown up and your wife is on her own. There's a sports club covering seventy-seven acres of the old Cobdown farm (the oast is part of the clubhouse), there is a nursery school, a couple of banks, doctors, dentists, chiropodists, five canteens, a visiting chaplain (the Revd Richard Lea), hairdressers, a sauna, and a supermarket. Reed International cares for its employees body and soul. When they die there will be a corner that is forever Reed reserved for them in heaven.

East Malling and Ditton and Aylesford may need Reed for the jobs it offers (though no more than other villages and less than Maidstone and the Medway towns), but it cannot be said that Reed needs East Malling and Ditton and Aylesford. It is a self-contained town. All the same, compared with allied industries, like the production end of Fleet Street, Reed has very few workers. Reed brings most kinds of tradesmen on from apprenticeship — bricklayers, electricians, plumbers, engineers — and only about a thousand of the work force are paper makers. The vast paper-making machines can be running and there will be perhaps two or three overalled figures around, watching dials or operating the machine that wraps the reels in brown paper. Only if something goes wrong does someone hit the panic button and men appear from nowhere.

So it isn't the number of men but the sheer scale of the operation that is impressive. Paper may begin its life as trees in a forest, but in the mill it starts as an evil-looking porridge fed from the pulp bales in the barges and the water of the mill stream and the Medway. By the time the porridge has been thinned and smoothed and cleaned out enough in the vat-like pulper, it begins its run along the conveyor belt, at the comfortingly untechnically-named wet end. When paper was handmade the stock (98 per cent water, the rest fibre) was put in a frame with a web of wire through which the water flowed and the fibres were retained. So it is here, except that the frame is a fast-moving belt of copper wire mesh. Most of the water drains through the mesh and the rest is dried out as the sheet of water turns magically into a white band of paper and gets squeezed between felt rollers first and then is run over heated rollers. And instead of a sheet of paper at a time, this paper runs off the end of the machine and reels itself into a vast 17-hundredweight cylinder.

Reg Spice had no difficulty choosing paper making as a career: his father was here before him and he too became chief paper maker. Mr Spice senior joined in the early 1920s when the firm was just expanding from the little mill in the village of Tovil to its narrow site between the railway line and the Medway, and beginning the process of transforming itself from humble Albert Reed Ltd, one of several small Kentish paper mills, to an international conglomerate which employs now 86,000 men in 40 countries and with a turnover of around £1,500 millions a year. Not that it has an untarnished tale of capitalist expansion and success: there was the trauma in the City of London because Reed apparently overreached itself in taking over a Canadian subsidiary. And there was the worldwide recession in the paper industry which at Reed Aylesford in 1971 meant cutting back from full capacity on thirteen machines to eight, and laying off a thousand workers. Now they are back up to nine and working at about 80 per cent capacity.

One question still sticks in Reg Spice's mind from his City and Guilds examination at the end of his apprenticeship in the early '50s: Where would you site a paper mill and why? You needed a river, rail, road, and local towns within a fourpenny bus ride, Reg Spice recalls, and Reed had it all.

Reed today squats on both sides of the Middle Cut on the Medway, which is tidal for another half-dozen miles upriver from here through Maidstone and towards Tonbridge. The railway that the London, Chatham & Dover built in 1856 runs through Reed territory for most of the mile between Aylesford and New Hythe stations through a deep cutting formed by mill walls. The London, Chatham & Dover built New Hythe station in railway Gothic by the Ferry Inn on the wharf. Now the ferry has gone, the inn stopped being a pub soon after the last war and became the Reed personnel department, and the railway station is practically a Reed franchise.

At the Aylesford entrance and at the New Hythe entrances there are security gates. But from time immemorial there has been a public footpath along the river front; Reed doesn't advertise it but it is still there. If you walk along it the chances are that at any given time there will be a dozen huge barges tied up at the wharf, loaded with pulp. When Reg Spice did his City and Guilds he pointed out that the Reed site fell short of perfection in one particular: there was no deep-water wharf. So the pulp for Reed comes to Rochester from the United States, from Canada, from Scandinavia, even a little from Spain; they unload it at Rochester and the Crescent Shipping Company brings it the rest of the way. Reed tries to unload it in time for the barges to return on the next tide, but sometimes they fall behind and the barges accrete upriver from the wharf, two dozen, three dozen, opposite the coal bunkers and the massive dusty-white concrete china-clay bunkers (the china clay comes from St Austell and Reed use 150 tons a week to close the gaps between the fibres in the paper and give it a finish). Downriver from the wharf there is a huge warehouse. Once it was an export warehouse for newsprint to the Continent. Now it is an import warehouse for pulp.

Nothing goes back down the river to Rochester. Since Reg Spice joined Reed the motorway has been built and everything goes out by road, thousands of tons of newsprint and packing paper and Kleenex tissues (from a corner of the site where Reed have a one-third interest in the New Hythe plant of the American firm, Kimberly Clark). The trucks thunder into London right through the day, all through the year, converging on the City through Deptford and Rotherhithe and the Old Kent Road and Southwark.

Past the china-clay bunkers and up the side of the sheer brick face of West Mill is an open wooden staircase — the Duke of Edinburgh steps, so called: built for a visit by the consort — up to a pedestrian bridge and pipeline a dizzy height above the river. The bridge connects with Reed International's latest pride and joy, the island site. From the bridge you look down on the river inlet, the marsh, and the stream that isolate the site from the high ground beyond. Then there are the big sludgy lagoons where the 600,000 gallons of water used every hour are cleaned and dumped back into the river (cleaner than they came out, Reg Spice says), a mill where used magazines and newspapers are pulped for re-use, and 12,000 tons of waste paper stacked in two yards. And every week a van from Whitehall draws up beside a chute leading into the mill; doors open up, Ministry men — bowler hats, pin stripes, umbrellas — leap out and monitor the action as the discarded secrets of Whitehall are loaded on to the chute and fed into the pulper. Reed spent around £6 millions on plant here, and it saved its newsprint manufacturing from extinction.

Reed started its new life by the Medway principally to make *Daily Mirror* paper. The *Mirror* put up a lot of the capital in 1921 and the first two machines made nothing but *Mirror* newsprint. But in the '60s and '70s the price of foreign pulp went through the ceiling. Reed technologists had been experimenting with ways of recycling paper and in 1964 they came up with a small plant which produced 15 tons of re-usable pulp a day at the Imperial Mills in Gravesend. Twenty-three hundredweight of waste paper will make a ton of pulp. There are great piles of *Woman*, *Woman's Own*, *Cosmopolitan*, *Woman's Home Journal*, old paperback books, and the seedier tit and bum publications. (A whole stack collapsed on a worker and killed him when he was ferreting around for his afternoon shot of soft porn. So now there is a rule forbidding workmen to remove magazines.) There are old wellington boots, bits of plastic, pieces of wire, broken bottles. The whole lot goes up the chute into a vat of water where a combination of centrifugal force, a barbed-wire-coated rope, and powerful jets of water separate the paper from the unwanted hardware. The ink is cleaned out, and what goes back through the pipeline over the bridge is an unappetising grey pulp, 98 per cent water.

Oddly enough this great feat of applied technology takes paper making back even closer to its origins, before the days of wood pulp, when the pioneers of the industry made their paper from rags. Apart from John Tomlin at Millhall (described as Paper Mill Farm in Abraham Walter's map of 1682–5), his contemporary and probable kinsman Roger Tomlyn of East Malling also had a paper mill when he died in 1704 ('Then I give, bequeath unto my loveing wife Mary Tomlyn All that my Messuage Millhouse paper mill drying houses implements thereunto belonging and lands with their appurtenances lying in East Malling in Kent').

The Tomlyns were a yeoman family of long standing in East Malling and in Ditton. They probably used their mills for grinding corn and perhaps for fulling cloth. Certainly one or two of the mills were used for fulling. *Valor Ecclesiasticus*, the report prepared by Thomas Cromwell's commission for Henry VIII on the sources of revenue of the monasteries, mentions 'Est Mallyng de proficuis molendini fullonici ibidem per annum £3.6s.8d.' *Molendini fullonici*: the first mention of fulling in East Malling. Since Malling Abbey's income from unspecified corn mills is reported as high as £19.17s.4d., it seems likely that the money was coming not just from the mill in West Malling and the corn mill in East Malling, but that the fulling mill in East Malling was grinding corn as well.

These were the skills that the Tomlyns knew. But in 1685 Louis XIV revoked the Edict of Nantes, which had given a measure of protection against religious persecution to the Huguenots. Among the thousands who fled to Kent were skilled paper makers, and it could be that the Tomlyns employed some of these. Like hop growing, paper making had existed before the foreigners arrived. Like hop growing, it now became one of Kent's growth industries, but operating alongside milling corn and fulling cloth. It was a cottage industry still, but it needed quantities of rags, and cutting off the buttons, tearing up the garments, and boiling them and stirring them to pulp was a filthy and thankless task which became a fit case for wage labour. And as the demand for paper grew, the mills became bigger and more specialised.

In East Malling it was made possible because, in common with the rest of England, the peasantry no longer existed: farmers hired wage labourers and laid them off when the weather was too bad for work or when the harvest was in. The habit of wage labour took hold, but the paths of the worker on the farm and the worker in the paper mill diverged.

For the farm labourer, old systems of patronage produced a form of loyalty that looks with hindsight unbelievable: even contemporary observers found it hard to imagine that England could continue through

the early years of the nineteenth century without a revolution. From the
end of the Napoleonic Wars East Malling's vestry records are a numbing
litany of relief applied for and given, or not:

*5 April 1818:* Mrs Wood for her daughter gone for service two shifts
and two aprons, granted. Mrs Hurley for three children 3 prs of half
boots. Two pr granted [on 26 June the vestry record shows Mrs Hurley
granted another pair of shoes].
   At a vestry held 10 April 1818 pursuant to public notice: Resolved,
that all persons in work shall bring a note from their master specifying
the money they have received before they are relieved by the overseer.
*30 October 1818:* Mr Knight in consideration for the loss of his wife's
hopping £4. Mr Shanks 2/6d. a week and necessary clothes. Robert
Leigh a Swans skin jacket 2 shifts 2 frocks 2 petticoats 2 pr of hose. Mr
Borner in consideration of sickness and loss of hopping £3, Mrs Good-
hugh's boy 2 shirts 2 pr of hose a swanskin jacket and trowsers.

And so on for eighteen entries.

*3 March 1820:* resolved that Thos Underhill shall be ordered to the
sitting to answer to his wages received from Mr Andrewes.
*5 May 1820:* Sir John Twisden, Bart., in the chair [this seems to have
been a rare honour]. Resolved to give E. Kemsley sufficient for a truss.
Resolved that Jas Gardner shall be made to pay his poor rates. Resolved to give Mr Oben a Round frock and a pr. of trowsers as an
encouragement.

And so on through the next decade. By 1831 the parish was falling back
on an old stratagem:

*18 May:* . . . for the purpose of considering the best method to employ
the poor at this season of the year there being many hands out of
employ, and other parochial business. It were resolved that the surveyor set men sufficient to put the footpath leading from East Malling
to West Malling in repairs immediately and the Road leading to
Newhithe and any other road that wants repairing.

By 23 April the following year, the year of the Reform Bill, the situ-
ation had become even more desperate and East Malling joined in the

clutch of parishes deciding to send some of its unwanted poor off to the colonies:

> . . . To consider the propriety of allowing money to persons belonging to the parish who may like to go to the British settlements in North America. It were agreed that the sum of £200 should be appropriated for the purpose of emigration and that a committee should be appointed to carry the same into fact. The following gentlemen were nominated to compose the committee [list of names appended]. It were agreed that 5 members should be a Quorum with power to act. It were resolved that a notice should be placed on the church doors stating a meeting will be held on Friday evening the 27th inst at 6 o'clock to receive the applications from any person desirous of emigrating.

It was a tough world in which strayed paupers were taken back under escort to their home parish so as not to be a burden on the ratepayers of their adopted home. Here, on 8 February 1801, is a churchwarden of Strood, on the opposite bank of the Medway from Rochester, writing to William Baker, overseer of East Malling's poor: 'Gentlemen, The bearer John Paine whome you Brought to Strood by A Removal Order, we do Acknowledge to be a Parishioner of Strood and are ready to Receive him or his family at any time, without expence to your Parish.'

In 1812 Dr George Perfect, the son of the first man to use electric shock treatment on mental patients, suffered the humiliation of signing a bastardy order whose pedantic phrasing has a certain remorseless beauty as it draws a legal noose tighter and inescapably tighter:

> Know all men by these presents that I George Perfect of West Malling in the County of Kent Surgeon am held and firmly bound to James Westbrook, William Terry, William Salmon, and Thurston Whittle, Churchwardens and Overseers of the Poor of the Parish of East Malling . . . in the sum of one hundred pounds of good and lawful money of Great Britain . . . I bind myself my heirs executors administrators and every one of them firmly by these presents sealed with my seal dated this first day of April in the fifty-second year of the reign of our Sovereign Lord George the Third by the Grace of God. . . . Whereas the above bound George Perfect is charged by Elizabeth Drew of East Malling aforesaid singlewoman to have had the carnal knowledge of her body and to be the putative father of a female and Bastard Child

lately born of her body which is (or is likely to be) chargeable to the Inhabitants of the said Parish. . . .

The point, of course, is the last phrase. Poverty and Poor Law relief was an obsession. Relief of the poor had been an obligation before the Conquest, and one which the Church carried through, however inefficiently, until the Reformation. Queen Elizabeth's Poor Law tried to remedy the chaos that followed, but by the nineteenth century the right of the poor to relief was increasingly resented and increasingly questioned. Ratepayers grudged subsidising the wage they felt farmers should be paying, and farmers pointed accusingly at the church and the lord of the manor, who still took their tithes of all produce.

Depression following the quick profits of the war years, the Corn Laws prohibiting imports, a flooded labour market with the discharge of Wellington's troops — all hit the nation hard, but at parish level the visible cause was tithes. Tithes had been with the parishes as long as poverty. The true story of the Twisdens is shown, not in the subdued splendour of Bradbourne, but in the building hidden behind the stable block, the tithe barn, rebuilt by the second baronet at the same time as the house itself. Its doors are huge enough to admit a fleet of double-decker buses; in those days, horse-drawn carts piled high with produce.

Yet these years passed without revolution. Cobbett stumped the country prophesying the holocaust to come, but in 1830 men forced by hunger to riot and burning and unlawful assembly stood by at the last and allowed their leaders, or supposed leaders, to be hanged and imprisoned and transported.

For the journeyman paper maker, things were different. He was a new servant to a new master. The John Larkings were entrepreneurs who through the century exploited fluid capital and the growth of joint-stock enterprise to make their fortunes. The number of mills in East Malling grew from two to four, one tailrace running almost straight into the next mill pond. It is the story of the industrial revolution writ small. John Larking's bank financed one paper maker (Balston) and Larking himself took up the innovations of another (Whatman's wove paper and bleached paper). The new entrepreneurism produced a new, extensive, leisured middle class and bodies of growingly trade- and class-conscious working men. While farm workers hung back, journeymen paper makers were in the forefront of the making of the English working class.

Already, before the dawn of the nineteenth century, John Larking and his colleague at Upper Mill, James Brooks, were worried by labour problems. In 1796 Parliament passed the Combination Acts, which were actually anti-combination acts. In 1799 and in most of the next five or six years Larking and Brooks met James Whatman and Thomas Balston of Maidstone and Thomas Golding of Ditton to decide on a course of action to outface the demands of their workers.

The confrontation between work force (combining illegally) and employers (free to combine) looks from our point of view radically modern. The workers picked off single employers or groups of employers and struck if need be; not just for money but for better working conditions, easier hours, meal breaks, compensation for loss of work. They were, already, a classical alienated working force. And in spite of the best efforts of Larking and his friends, the journeymen paper makers inexorably improved their lot.

In 1803 the masters met at the Bull in Rochester (where Charles Dickens later had Mr Pickwick and his friend Mr Tupman stay) and tried to buy off trouble by setting out a code of practice that would have given workers from 19s.2d. a week to £1.4s.6d. a week according to the skills of the worker and the grade of paper being manufactured, with a guaranteed six-day week, an extra 1s. a week where beer was not supplied during working hours, and a sick fund. The work force refused this offer, presumably because the proposals also stipulated the employment of one apprentice to a vat: a potential source of blackleg labour. There must as well already have been a history of mutual suspicion, not surprising after the Combination Acts (and the master paper makers' agreement specifically banned employment for members of workmen's 'clubs'). The habit of patronising workmen was deeply ingrained: appropriate, perhaps, when the workman was a farm labourer living with the farmer and his family, wholly inappropriate to the often-nomadic journeymen paper makers, though the habit has persisted in some areas of labour relations to this day.

But the figures in the wage proposal give some idea of the expectation of the paper worker in a growing trade. Agricultural workers meanwhile were being thrown on the parish wholesale to make up a living wage, and even when they could get full-time work the average wage (though such national figures as exist are patchy and disputed) seems to have been only 8s. or 9s. a week (wives might bring in another 4s. or 5s.; but the same was true of paper workers' wives). By 1820 East Malling vestry 'resolv'd that Mr Chittenden's money should be made up to 15s.', suggesting that this might be a reasonable wage had he been able to work full time.

John Larking, as a landowner as well as an entrepreneur, was engaged both in paying his own labour force in the paper mill and also in subsidising the poor agricultural worker of East Malling. The parish poor rate of 1800–1 was levied at 5s. in the pound. Larking received £293.10s. in rent and paid £73.7s.6d. for the poor rate; James Brooks received £151 in rent and paid out £37.15s. (Sir John Twisden meanwhile received £322.10s. in rent and paid £80.12s.6d.; but he also paid £34.7s.6d. on his corn tithe valued at £137.10s.).

From the Poor Law of 1834, which lifted the burden from the parish without immediately improving the lot of the labourer, to the welfare state of the second half of the twentieth century, the old distinction between farm worker and industrial worker has persisted: compare the £40 or £50 a labourer at Broadwater might earn for a variety of skills from handling machines to handling pesticides, to the average £76 at Reed for a single skill — driving a fork-lift or minding a machine.

Reed and Kimberly Clark, visible for miles around from the high North Downs above the Medway, are the outward sign of a process of disintegration that started when John Larking arrived in East Malling and turned a craft into an industry. The gain in well-being and the destruction of poverty are not to be denied, but something has been lost as well. By 1817 Larking's own business was in trouble; he had fled and his land was held in trust. But the Busbridges followed him and introduced vast new paper-making machines. The Education Acts of the late nineteenth century produced a new mass literacy. By the end of the century the paper makers needed vast imports of foreign wood pulp to meet the demand for more and more really white paper. One East Malling mill was already closed, the others obsolescent.

The ghost of Abraham Walter, surveyor and map maker, hangs over Millhall as over everything else in this book. His map of Paper Mill Farm shows 'House, Orchard, yards, & Mill-pond, 1 acre 2 rods; A Slip by ye Pond Side, 1 rod 26 perches; Barnfield, 1 acre 1 rod 21 perches; Way Field, 3 acres 21 perches'. There are twenty-six timber elms and twelve young elms and two young ashes. As you drive towards London on the M 20 you might just glimpse the glint of light on water. That's what's left of the mill pond. The motorway has obliterated the rest.

# 7 The railway came through the middle of the house

**We've lorst all the big ones now.**   Cecil John Chambers

THIS CHAPTER IS devoted to Cecil John Chambers. There is no point in trying to feed his words into the general narrative because he tells better than I could what it was like to live in East Malling towards the end of the nineteenth century and in the early years of this century. There are others like him in the parish: an old woman at New Hythe who has never seen the motorway two hundred yards from her front door, another who lives in a cottage fifty yards from where she was born. But there is no one whose memory goes as far back.

Mr Chambers's father was Jabez John Chambers, the village butcher. Cecil was born in the room above the butcher's shop in Mill Street. Apart from spending the years 1914–19 at war, Mr Chambers has lived no-where else. He learnt his trade as a carpenter in the old carpenter's shop by the station and he spent most of his working life at Malling Abbey.

It is difficult and perhaps foolhardy to try to preserve dialect in print, but the survival of the Kentish burr and idiom so close to London is a miracle. Not long ago, before British Rail installed bland standard English train announcements, there was a railway porter who announced trains in a broad Kentish accent as close to London as Swanley Junction, last stop before suburbia. Some of the young men on the farms retain the accent, but the closeness of London is intruding. Anyway, since I have retained Mr Chambers's figures of speech, I have tried intermittently to indicate pronunciation as well.

A couple of months after we had this conversation Mr Chambers died. He was ninety-six.

*What was the village like when you were a boy?*
They had the fair in 1885 on the green. We called it a fair that time o' day you know, but people would have laughed at it now, to see a man turning a handle to make the roundabout go around. Sitting in boxes. There warn't no war memorial then you see. Course, years ago, the tradesmen what got 'orses used to take em up there and they had that stream for to wash their carts. Y'see, that piece belonged to Twisden. They're a very old family you know. I knew the last one and the daughters

too. There was two of them. They weren't married. I did do a bit of carving for them. She wanted a little bit done, I said all right, I'll do it for you. It was a bit orf a chair I think, orf a chair. It got broken, it'd got to be ornamented the same as the others.

Then you see there was W. L. Wigan, down the road here. Clare Cottage. I worked there. 'E wasn't the vicar. I should think that would be his father, Septimus Wigan. We've lorst all the big ones now. There was Twisden, and Wigan, and Mercer. Mercer. Had a big farm over Well Street, Broadwater. Terrible lot of 'op gardens he had over there, Mercer. They just moved, the Mercers did. The son, he just moved right out of East Malling. The Wigans, there ain't no Wigans in East Malling now; the daughter, she was the last one. I don't know where she's gone. Down in the shires somewhere.

*Do you remember the station opening up here, the railway halt?*

The halt? Yes. The first train stopped here, let's see, twenty, thirty, forty, fifty, sixty, seventy . . . well, somewhere about, er, sixty years ago the first train stopped there. I remember seeing it. The eight o'clock train come. And we come out — that was where our carpenter's shop was, just above there — and the men come out at eight o'clock to go home to breakfast, and I was with them and that train stood on the bridge. That did look funny, the first time. The fare used to be threepence, I think, to Maidstone, and fourpence from West Malling to Maidstone. Then Queen Victoria, she come through 'ere in 1900. I think she died in 1901 when the Boer War was over. The Boer War was in 1901. I hadn't finished me training when that ended so I didn't 'ave to go. King Edward took the throne, didn't he. A few days before he was crowned he had appendicitis. And he wasn't crowned, not till August. 'Cos I was in the Medicals, when they were going to 'ave the Coronation, I went up with a gang, all our lot went up to line the streets for accidents, you know, red crorss. Well then we had to come away, nothing doing 'cos they cancelled the Coronation. I believe it was appendicitis he had, two days before he was supposed to be crowned. 'E was getting on then. You see, when he died King George, he took the place. I met him out in France, a place called Senlis, just outside of Albert. He come out there, just to have a look round.

*What happened when the Queen went through East Malling?*

One engine went through first. What the men told me was, it was what they called the pilot engine. That was to see that the track was all clear. Then the other one, the royal train, came through just afterwards. And my boss, he was a very very good chap, 'cos the ground run close to the railway, we put some trestles up, and boards, so we could stand up high beside the embankment and look into her carriage. He took a lot of pains with that.

*How many of you were there watching?*

Oh, the man, and his wife, the two daughters, and the son. At that time o' day it was only sixpence an hour. That's all we got then, sixpence an hour. From six o'clock in the morning till half-past five at night. Half-hour breakfast, and from one to two, dinner. None of that now. That's what it was, sixpence an hour. Every day. Leave off twelve o'clock Saturday. We didn't have no week's holidays. No, if we had a week's holiday you got to lose a week's money. No, no holiday time.

*How did sixpence an hour compare with what other people got in the village, like on the farms?*

Well, their money would be about twenty-three or -four shillings. Some of them only got about eighteen shillings. A builder's labourer, he got four-pence an hour, a builder's labourer. We used to live very nice. I just bought a half ounce o' tobacco now, it was eight bob. Well, that time o' day half a ounce of tobacco would have been twopence. And you could buy five cigarettes for a penny. And you could get a glass of ale for three ha'pence. I used to have a glass of beer occasionally, but I wasn't a big public house man. If I had beer the publican would bring it down here. Or you could take the jug and go and get a pint of beer. No bottles or nothing like that. You'd have it in a jug, go'n get a pint of beer. Down at the King and Queen. You see, our village is royalty. King and Queen down there, and the Prince of Wales just underneath the bridge. A man named Bottle had the Prince of Wales for years. And the Ship's been altered. When they built the railway, they had to pull a bit of the Ship down to let the railway come straight through. So they built another bit on it afterwards.

*What sort of transport was there around here then apart from the trains?*

None at all. When I got the children me and the missus used to push the children into Maidstone and think nothing of it. Down by the Research. No, there was no motor. You could get a ride: used to be a man named Brown used to come through, what they called a carrier. Then if you wanted anything in Maidstone, you'd tell him or give him the paper and he'd go to that shop and get it for you and bring it home and charge you threepence or fourpence. And if you wanted to ride into Maidstone he'd give you a ride into Maidstone for sixpence. It'd take you about an hour and a half to go in.

*There weren't enough shops in East Malling I suppose?*
No. That bottom one, the guest house, was a grocer's shop. There was four bakers. Two of them in Chapel Street. The one that's still there over the road. And one in Mill Street, the motorbike shop now. You can see the oven out the back. By the green it was a big grocer's shop. People by the name of Pearce had it. Well, it warn't Pearce first. It was a Miss Millin. But then a chap she had working in the shop was named Pearce, and she married him. And he was about twenty-one or twenty-two and she was about forty-two. And that didn't answer. He played merry hell with her when he got the money and made her go bankrupt. And then she struggled on again, got round a bit, got her discharge, then she started over there. And they sent 'im to Canada, and that's where he stopped . . . well, he's been dead some years now, but never come back no more.
*What were the roads like?*
The roads? Oh cripes. Years ago there used to be an old man they'd have down the road here, they'd pour great big lumps of stone out of those half-a-bushel baskets, and then they had this old man what they call a stonebreaker and he used to break it up into smaller bits then they used to lay it down on the road, then they used to throw dirt over it and then a horse and cart would come along, and then a steamroller to roll it down. Wor, but it was rough. They'd throw this muck down, then water it, and then the roller used to go up and down. That's how they used to make the roads that time o' day. Not like they do now.

Then the traction engines used to come up through here you see. The farmer up here, Mercer, used to have manure come down to New Hythe wharf from London, you know, from the stables up in London. And then a traction engine would load up with three trucks and come up through here to the farm. And then a man used to have to walk in front, 'cos occasionally they'd meet horses, so the man in front used to have to lead the horse by the traction engine. Hayman and Porter was most of the engines, from Rochester. The old steam engines. Then there was what we called the ploughing engine. That was a very big engine. There used to be two engines, one up that end of the field, and one up that. And they had a long chain and a big plough on it. That one up there would pull it up that way, this one would pull it back the other way. What they call a plough engine. Oh, they used to do a devil of a lot at a time.
*How long have you lived in this house now?*
Erm, 1920. I used to live down Church Street. You know that antique shop? Next door to that. That's where I lived first, yes, when I was, after

I got married, my father and mother, they had the shop, then they retired and they went down to Larkfield to live and then moved into Maidstone. That's where I lived, next door to that antique shop. All this house, property, belonged to Father, my father. Then when he died he left it all to me.

It used to go in the name of Huggett's Farm, because that time o' day there used to be a man live here named Huggett and he had cows, out in this meadow. And he used to go round with the milk. And they called it Huggett's Farm. But it's not a farm. That time o' day they didn't have milk bottles. A man used to come round with two big churns, one in each hand. And he'd put it down. Pint o' milk you'd want. He'd open the lid and make you out a pint. He was the only one in East Malling that time o' day. Then it warn't half the people in East Malling there is at the present time. There weren't no house down the park for a start. That was all arable. Man named Matthews had it, for his cows. Then them 'ouses over the road here, they weren't built. They were built when I went to school. Used to be ninety of us to go to school there. Now down here there's about a hundred and ninety.

*What was school like in those days?*

I believe we had to pay threepence a week. I believe we paid threepence a week every Monday morning. I don't know what that was for, for the funds I suppose. Threepence.

*How many teachers did they have up there?*

Three or four. And the master. A man named Moorland. He was the schoolmaster when I was there. He retired and took a public house up at Rochester. His wife, she hung herself up there at the school. And he retired then. Went up to Chatham, Rochester or Chatham, took a public house up there. Then he got married, to one of the teachers. Named Miss Durrell her name was.

*How old were you when you left school?*

Fourteen. Not many days after I was fourteen I said to Father, I'm fourteen now, I can leave school. Aw, good idea, I mortally hated school you know. Oh cripes. He said if you leave school I'll see you don't run about in the streets, he said, you start work. He said I don't know what you want to be.

*Didn't he want you in his business?*

No. No. I had three brothers, they went all butchers. But I didn't, I never took to butchery. I wanted to be an engine driver. You see, all my mother's people were on the railway  Her father was an inspector on the railway, and all her brothers and all their children were all on the railway. One of the sons was station master at Wateringbury. And another one at Ashford. And another one, he worked at Ashford works. They've all been on the railway, and that's what I wanted to do but Father said, No, you don't want a dirty job like that. And he says, the man up the street, Butterick the builder, he wants an apprentice. You go there. I says yes, I'll go there, so's never to go back to school. So I says, yes, I'll take it. But for three or four months it didn't suit me a bit. Only the other carpenter said, oh, you stick it mate, you'll be all right presently. I says well, I hope so.

I learned pretty quick. When I worked at the Abbey, over the doorways and that was a lot of carving, and then I'd perhaps have to take something down and make it correspond to that bit. When I was there, there was between thirty and forty nuns. I was there thirty-five years. I come out of the army in 1919. Before I went to the Abbey, I was waiting four years in the army. I left England in March 1915, and went to the Dardanelles. Turkey. Anzac.

*It was a disaster, wasn't it?*

Yeh. Had to give it up. Then when I come 'ome, after, at the beginning of 1916, I went to France. In the Royal Ingineers. Yes, I went right through, right from Albert right up to Ypres. It were all walking, no motoring. When we had to shoot the Jerrys we used to walk about three days to one place. Then stop there so long, then orf again. Do what we got to do there then clear orf again.

In the Second War I'd carve sitting right here at that table. I was a special constable. And then if the sireen went or I was on duty that night, if I was on duty whether there was a sireen or not I'd got to go out. Then I'd sit here do a little bit of carving. Then after I'd done it I gave it to the people at the church down Paddock Wood. And I give them a candlestick. And you know West Malling church? You ever been inside that? You seen them candlesticks round the altar? I made all four o' them. And I made one candlestick for the church in the Tonbridge road. And I made a oak flower pedestal for Barming church. I used to do it to pass the time away. I want to do three or four jobs now, only I can't see until I get my glasses. That's what I'm waiting for. There's a lot of pencil work. Line.

*What did other people in the village work at when you were young?*

Oh, different things.

*Mills?*

Yes, they had two paper mills here. The paper mills and the flour mill. Well all the men used to work in the mills. And the women too, a lot of the women. They had what they call the rag mill, where they used to make paper out of rags. Well, it's all shut up now. They wouldn't look at a place like this now. Not big enough. No. But it was that time o' the day. Years ago when my mother and father lived down there, they had a man, a lodger, and he was in charge of the banknote paper what they made down there. They made a lot of banknote paper. It had to be special paper, and it had to be special silk, to make 'em. That was a very old family, the Busbridges. That used to belong to them. They lived over Malling but the works were here. Then the flour mill, that belonged to a man named Phillips. He had those houses built over there, the other side of the High Street, for it was Phillips wot had all these hop gardens up on the Rocks. It was hop garden from here right up to the top. Now there ain't no hop gardens at all; all fruit trees. Ain't many hop gardens about now. Wotsisname down Yalding, he did away with a lot of hops. I don't think they put a lot of hops in beer now do they? Adulterated. See a lot of the brewers, Fremlins at Maidstone, they finished up. Whitbread, he's the biggest one now. It's Whitbread wot has the farm at Yalding. Hop farms there, but he's done away with a lot of his hops. When I was a boy there was a odd-job man called Charlie, had a brother called Tom who worked at the paper mill. Caught one hand in the machinery, and tried to pull it out with the other. Lost both hands. He had hooks instead. I used to hang a box of sweets around Tom's neck in hopping time for him to go round the fields selling them to mothers for their children.

You used to have to make seven bushels when my missus and me went hopping and then you got a shilling. Yeh, you'd got to work 'ard for seven bushels, then you got a shilling. And if you picked twenty bushels in a day, you were doing jolly fine, if you earned three bob. Yeh, my missus, she used to go hop picking.

We got married down there, East Malling church. I was christened there, I was confirmed there, and I was married there. So was the missus. She's lived in East Malling all her life. We're both old hands. She's ninety-two now. Me ninety-six.

I never retired till I was seventy. That was a very nice place to work for anybody. Oh yes. They don't rush you. They'd say can I have that at a certain time. Oh yes, that'd be all right. Long as you get that done that's all right. You ain't got to rush over it. My money over there was only £5.10s. a week. When I retired, my money was only £5.10s. a week. A lot of chaps used to say, I wouldn't stop there, I'd go and earn more money than that. And then I used to say, I know where I'm best orf.

I was satisfied with my money, and I reckon that's what it is makes me like I am. I've never overdone it, not to earn a extra shilling. I been satisfied with what they paid me. And I tell anybody else if they done the same, they'd be the same. I haven't had no illnesses, but I always put it down that I didn't tear me inside out trying for a extra shilling. You take a bloke on piece work and all that, he's crocked up by the time he's seventy. Whereas meself, I don't say I can do hard work, I can't. But I can do carpentering, and I can tell yer how to do a job. That was my last job, making that door. No, they were jolly nice people at the Abbey. I buried every one, whilst I was there. Buried every one whilst I was working there. Used to make the coffin in my shop. Had a nice workshop. Well it's still there, beautiful workshop. There was about thirty or forty nuns there when I worked there. They never come out, you know, never come out on the streets, they stop there all the time. It's been a Abbey years and years. I tell you, Gundulf, I think, was the architect of that, and he was the architect of Rochester Cathedral, and they was built at the same time, or nearly the same time, I've heard them say. But they've added to it a lot since they've been there. You know that barn over at Water Lane? They've turned that into a chapel. You know what the name of that barn is? Buggery barn. I don't know how it got that name. You ask anybody in West Malling and they'll tell you it's called Buggery barn. But it's a chapel now. But it was a big old barn. Tithes wasn't it? Tithe barn. I believe there's some monks live there now. See, when the Second War broke out, all the nuns, they cleared out down to the shires, I've forgotten the name of the place now. I was down there two or three weeks, doing the alterations, Yes, they cleared out two or three days after war was declared. You'd have thought they'd have stopped at the Abbey with their religion, wouldn't you? Well, they didn't. Devonshire way I believe it was, because they used to have a public house, and it was a glass of cider, Devonshire cider. Because I had to lodge in the public house. Fitting up the place, it was a big old house, been empty a long time. Then when I came home they wouldn't let me go back because they made me join the police. I got to do something that was of national importance. There was about six or eight of us and we used to work in pairs. Not in daytime, but if it was at night, after about six o'clock or seven o'clock, you used to have to parade all round to see that there was no lights shining, all round the village. They dropped a bomb over in the

Research and the blast come right through to a window next door and blowed it out and that chimney what you see sticking up out there, it cracked it right down. They had to pull the chimney down and rebuild it. And that was oh, nearly half a mile away. But they dropped one in the Abbey grounds when I was there, but it didn't do a lot of damage, only blowed the windows out. Being soft ground it buried itself in and then exploded. But he dropped another one at the top of the town and that killed four or five, and then he come down and dropped one in the Abbey, and then he come down to Luck's Hill on the way to West Malling and he dropped one there. They were after him, see, and he wanted to get rid of them and he dropped them anywhere. He dropped one on the aerodrome. Then we had one of them doodlebugs. That dropped up the Heath. In a field. Didn't hurt no one.

I used to ride a bike to the Abbey when I went to work first of all. Not like the first bike in East Malling. An engineer at the mill made that, all wood, no pedals. Had to push it with his feet. Then when I come out of the army I bought myself a motorbike and sidecar to take the missus. Well, that went on for some little time and I said, not likely, if it rains we'd both be wet through. So I bought the car, let's see, yes, secondhand, and that's the clock out of it, there, on the mantelpiece. I made that with them elephants. There's the other elephant up there on the dresser. There used to be three elephants on it. Me first car, Morris. Gentleman lived down the road here, he was going away, he wanted to get rid of it. I think he charged me £30 for it. I kept it a long time, only it was all open. If it rained you got wet through. We ended up in the rain once, I said we'll get rid of it. And I sold that and bought another one, a saloon one. And I sold that just a few years ago, and I sold it for more than I give for it. That was a Morris, a Morris Ten. I had my first car in 1921 or '2. Then I had to give it up in 1960. Yeh, 1960 when I drove my car last. Then I drove it into the garage and my youngest boy said That's the last time you're going to have that car out dad. He said no more driving for you. He says you're too old. So I had to sell it. But I took that clock out of me first car, the other one's in there. I didn't put elephants round it. I put three elephants round that one only the missus, she said, I don't like that elephant up there on top, she says, take it off. I had to take it off.
*Did she use to work at the Abbey as well?*
No she never worked after we got married.
*Was she working before you got married?*
No, no. She had to work at home with her mother, she hadn't got a father.

Her mother was a invalid, so she had to stop at home. Then when her mother died we got married. I think we got married around about 1909. I think I'd been married about four years or something like that, five years, before the First War. I think it was 1909 when I got married, 1910 ... I wouldn't like to say. Someone told me one day, you had a diamond jubilee, I said I don't know, I don't know about it.

# 8 In their infinite wisdom

**For forms of government let fools contest,
Whate'er is best administered is best.**   Alexander Pope

*Abraham Walter's own farm at Larkfield from his maps of the Twisden Estate*

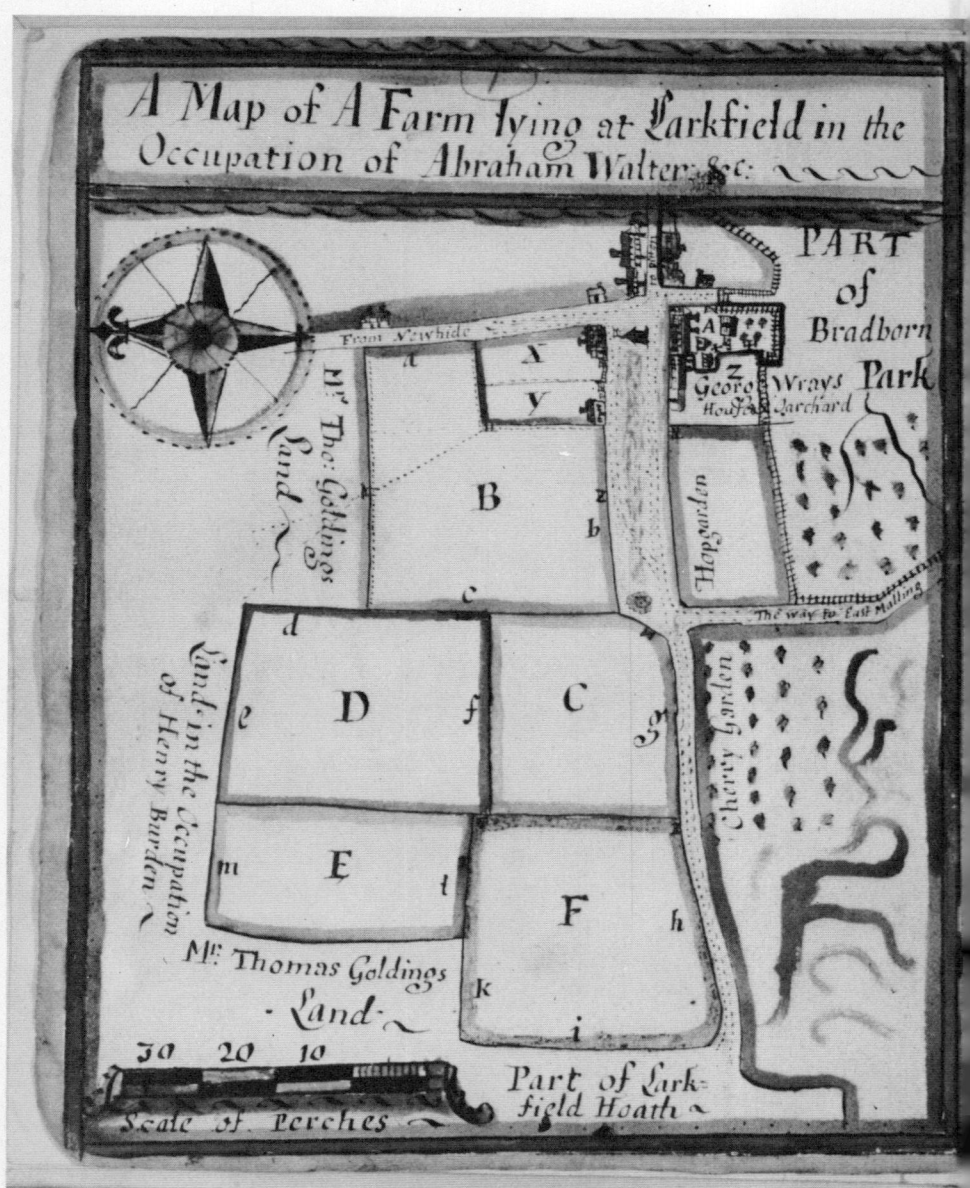

IT IS EARLY May, the time when government becomes accountable to the people. All over England and Wales the 7,800 parish and community councils are laying themselves bare before the electorate. They are holding the annual parish meetings at which the public may cross-examine their elected representatives. Council and committee meetings through the year are open to the public, and if a parishioner comes along with a grievance about an allotment or about planning permission for a garage,

| The Contents of the Land | Ac: R: P: |
|---|---|
| A:  The Houfe, yard, & Oarchard | 0 — 2 — 10 |
| B:  The Green Field | 6 — 0 — 20 |
| C:  The Pond Field | 4 — 0 — 13 |
| D:  The Great Quickfet | 6 — 0 — 04 |
| E:  The Little Quickfet | 3 — 1 — 08 |
| F:  The Hoath Field | 5 — 3 — 37 |
| Summe of Acres | 26 = 0 = 12 |

**Explation of Notes in ỹ Map**

X: Is Mr Thomas Goldings Plott of ground with his Houfe & Barn standing thereon; (Y) is Edmund Wallers Plott of ground & his Houfe & Shop ~~ Z) is George Wray's Plott of ground with his Houfe Maulthoufe & Barn ~ ) The Court-houfe Standing on Larkfield-green, Being the place where the Court is held & Constables chofen for ỹ Hundred of Larkfield ——— Boundary Lines, Signifying that thofe Fences are not maintained by this Land ~ ✠) Stands in the Table of Trees and the like (✠) may be found in ỹ Plott of the Houfe and Oarchard: And fhews that in the Fence between the Oarchard & yard & George Wrays Oarchard there is :6: Timber Elms, 7: Pollard Elms, and two Afhes &c: ~~~~

**Table of Trees**

| | Tim Elm | Poll Elm | Yeog Elm | Poll oak | Ash |
|---|---|---|---|---|---|
| ✠ | 6 | 7 | — | | 2 |
| a | 4 | 24 | — | | 2 |
| b | 6 | 15 | 3 | — | |
| c | 16 | 18 | 14 | — | 1 |
| d | 7 | 10 | 2 | | |
| e | 7 | 2 | 12 | | |
| f | 4 | 9 | 3 | 1 | 1 |
| g | 3 | 2 | 2 | — | 3 |
| h | 10 | 2 | — | 2 | 24 |
| i | 1 | 2 | 12 | 3 | 9 |
| k | 7 | 10 | — | | |
| l | 1 | 5 | — | | |
| m | — | 5 | - | 1 | 3 |
| n | 72 | 311 | 48 | 7 | 45 |

he will even be invited to speak; but the annual parish meeting is the one occasion when broad matters of policy can be thrashed out by council and public. That, anyway, is the theory.

In East Malling this year there are a couple of added inducements. The chairman of the council, David Thornewell, is a young solicitor's clerk who has lived in Larkfield all his life, on the London Road in a cottage opposite the north wall of Bradbourne. He knows every footpath, every hedgerow, every boundary stone, and he remembers a lot of what went when Government policy decreed the Medway Gap as a development area and the fields and meadows north of the London Road were buried in bricks and mortar and tarmac. He is a utilitarian amateur photographer, and he has recorded the passing of rural Larkfield. So before the meeting there is a small exhibition of his photographs, with old Ordnance Survey maps and a six-inch-to-the-mile map marked out with every public footpath and its number. And then there is a star attraction as well, a lady from the Kent Trust for Nature Conservation, with a set of colour slides of Kent flora and fauna.

At eight o'clock the parish clerk starts the meeting. The parish population is around 11,000. Two dozen electors have turned up. And many of them are councillors. The trouble is that now, people know, the power has fled from the manor, from the vestry, from the parish, to trade unions, to the shop floor, to the law courts, to employment and rent tribunals, to bigger units of government centred on Maidstone and Whitehall and their factotums in Bootle and Swansea. People know this and they neglect their rights as parishioners. And yet, the curious thing is that since people became more concerned about the nature of their village, about preserving its unity and character, the parish council has acquired a voice. As district and county and regional and national government has become more remote, the parish has remained the one part of government with a human face.

Parish councils do not have ministries or departments of paid experts making sure the oils are wheeled and the decisions are implemented. Partly, this is by design. When the Local Government Act of 1972 recast the whole shape of local government, it actually introduced new statutory functions for the parish councils. These did not amount to powers, but they gave the parish an effective voice — or rather, a more effective voice — in governing what happened within its own boundaries. The Act came into effect on April Fool's Day, 1974, so the worst might have been expected.

East Malling Church

Mill Street, East Malling: (*above*) *c.* 1900, private hop garden
in the background; (*below*) 1979, now a private garden

In the same parish: (*above*)
Reed International—as old as
Albert Reed; (*below*) Weir
Mill, as old as Domesday

Springhead, where the mill stream rises: the source
of the village's living

The boundaries of East Malling and Larkfield Civil Parish are by and large the same as the ancient ecclesiastical parish of East Malling, when Holy Trinity was merely a chapel of ease to St James's. But now East Malling and Larkfield are reckoned to have something like parity: Larkfield, the bigger north ward which includes New Hythe, returns eight members to the council, East Malling itself, the south ward, returns seven. The hardiest perennial among council topics is whether to follow the Church and make the two wards of the parish two separate parishes; but partly from sentiment, more obviously for reasons of parish-pump *Realpolitik*, every time the subject crops up the council decides to retain such muscle as it has as a single large unit.

The same Parliamentary Act made Tonbridge Rural Council and Malling Rural Council into Tonbridge and Malling District Council, the same size as the Parliamentary constituency. This council has its equivalent to Westminster's leader of the House and Westminster's party whips. The informality has fled, and two of the three parish councillors who also serve on the district council, David Thornewell and Bernard Pollock, prefer the parish council for its amateurishness and the sense that decisions are implemented by the councillors themselves, not by trained bureaucrats. There they can push to modify a planning decision about separating pedestrians and cars on a new housing estate (Thornewell) or to have a family rehoused or a widow found a place in an old people's home (Pollock). They may involve themselves in politics — no one locally doubts that the Liberals are the people who push hardest and publicise themselves best by championing individuals against the felt persecution of faceless bureaucracy, and there are Liberals on the parish council, among them the three district councillors and some others who actually vote differently at national level — but just as there are no experts to run things, only a part-time clerk, so there are no party politics in the village hall.

The parish clerk is a compact Welshman called Bryn Terrell. He wears a small, faintly military moustache and sports a sardonically deferential manner which runs to turns of phrase like 'in their infinite wisdom', which he normally deploys about decisions by his council or by professional planners. The irony does not hide an evident enjoyment of people and their political behaviour, in the broadest sense; nor does his pleasure in anticipating the wishes of the council and getting things done conceal the sense that he is there to serve. Like many of his kind, council officials and magistrates' clerks (the trained lawyers who advise lay

justices on their powers), he manages his council and occasionally he
makes a small display of it, but mostly he is as unobtrusive as can be.

He learnt diplomacy as a schoolmaster in Southampton. Local government came after retirement: he didn't like going rusty, saw the advertise-
ment, and applied. He made it his business when he moved into the job
to learn the broad provisions of the 1972 Local Government Act and he
keeps a copy of the Act at his elbow. It is an uncommon day when a
councillor catches him out on one of the statutes.

Bryn Terrell runs his council with five committees, called Allotments
and Open Spaces, Amenities (street lighting and footpaths), Finance and
General Purposes, Planning and Development, and Village Halls
Management. Five councillors sit on each committee with two co-opted
members of the public on all but the Finance and General Purposes Committee, which by law must consist of councillors alone. The council functions on an annual budget of around £30,000 and each of the committees
can spend up to £100 on a single project. If it wants to spend more, it has
to send the proposal through to the Finance Committee, so any large
expenditure will have gone through three forums by the time the council
itself nods the proposals through, or not, at its monthly meeting.

There was a time after the war when Labour controlled the parish
council, but as more private houses were built in the parish the face of
local politics changed. The Liberals produce a cyclostyled sheet called
*Hotline* which deals on a broadly non-partisan basis with local issues and
has attracted support from a mixed bag of people. Doris Wise, for one.
She runs her own hairdressing shop on the Clare Park estate and, like a
lot of country folk including her parents, she has voted Tory all her life.
She was born in Tonbridge and lived in East Peckham before she came
to East Malling, and had never been in local government before. But six
six years ago she decided she ought to do her bit, stood for the council,
and was elected. She stood as a Liberal because she had met Liberals
locally and they were the ones who were not only concerned about issues,
but did something about them. 'I'll give you a f'rinstance,' she says. 'A
young couple came to see me. He had come out of the army from Ger-
many with his wife and he went to the district council about somewhere
to live, and they said Oh dear, we've forgotten all about you. There's no
doubt that he had written to them, and he had a copy of the letter from
his commanding officer to the council saying that he was coming out of
the army with nowhere to live. He came to me and I spoke to David

Thornewell, and he advised me what to do. I told the young couple, you must keep going back to the council, don't let them get away with it. And we got on to the council too. That was Friday. On Monday the couple were given a place to live. The Liberals will help anyone.'

Animosity towards the district council is a recurring motif, maybe because they are the most accessible larger authority and the most responsive. Towards the county council and the Department of the Environment resentment is tempered by a feeling of helplessness: the big boys push the small ones around and there isn't much of a way of getting back at them. The current planning orthodoxy in Kent County Hall is that the Medway Gap villages need a big shopping centre. There is no apparent desire in the Medway Gap for a shopping centre; on the contrary, the county council withdrew in confusion in the face of unexpectedly vocal and well-organised protests from the villagers of Leybourne, the first site suggested. Now it has settled on Larkfield and again it is ignoring parish council arguments — that the shopping centre is not wanted, would put small shopkeepers out of business, would bring unwanted traffic, and would be a blemish — in favour of the purity of its planning concept.

But district council does respond quite often and is in frequent, almost daily, touch with Bryn Terrell. It has a presence that can be attacked. Peter Kilner is the only one of the three parish councillors also on the district council who actually prefers district affairs; and he is a marketing manager for Kimberly Clark (the American manufacturers of Kleenex tissues with a mill in New Hythe), young, smart, personable, coherent, and commanding, the kind of man who would make a mark anywhere and who would be attracted to the greater challenge of a bigger authority.

He came to Larkfield six years ago and began to realise that it was being built up without any cohesive forethought; it had been listed as suitable for development, so it would get development, piecemeal. He was in his thirties, living close to his place of work, and began feeling it was time he put something into the community. A friend was leaving the area and over dinner one night the two discussed the question of Kilner taking his place in local government. Like Kilner, the friend was a Liberal voter. Kilner liked his approach, stood for parish and district council and was elected for both. 'Quite honestly,' he says, 'I prefer district council. It is more structured. One feels that a meeting is getting somewhere.' At the first meeting of the new Village Hall Committee that replaced two previous committees (one for East Malling's hall, one for

Larkfield's), Bryn Terrell had taken an evening off because his volunteer assistant looks after village hall correspondence and bookings. It was Peter Kilner who cut through the chaos of attempts to dovetail the affairs of the two committees, and imposed some sort of shape and order on the proceedings.

One parish councillor who finds district council as remote as county council is Brenda Hawker. She got up a head of steam over what she felt was a personal battle with Tonbridge and Malling council. They were steamrollering through a measure to build a car park at the back of her parents' council house in Clare Park estate. That was two years ago and she was unmarried at the time, working for Maidstone council. So she knew the ropes and felt confident in taking Tonbridge and Malling on. 'I realised money was being spent without reference back to anybody who it affected,' she says. She spoke to a number of district councillors and the Liberals decided to take up her cause. Between them they killed the idea of a car park and Brenda Hawker stood at the district and parish council elections; she made it to the parish council but not to district. Soon after she was married and had a baby, so now she finds parish council a fulfilling alternative to being a housewife and is relieved that she wasn't elected to the district.

The newest parish councillor, Jean Lovering, agreed to serve because she was fed up with the way district council was dealing with — or rather, failing to deal with — a neighbourhood boundary dispute, involving a newcomer fencing the source of a stream that had always been reckoned common land. The dispute had been long and complicated and when she telephoned the district council she was, she thought, treated rudely. 'I thought, we pay these people. And I asked around the place about how I could get on to the parish council.' She had five children, all grown up, two of them at university, so she had time on her hands. She was already a governor of Clare Park secondary school, and now she had herself co-opted as one of the two public members of the Village Hall Committee. She let it be known that she would like to be a councillor, and when George Holding, council chairman at the time, died of a heart attack, she was picked by the council out of three applicants for the seat. (Parish councils can have by-elections, but it's an expensive business printing up the voting forms so East Malling prefers to co-opt.) She is one of the four Independents. 'If I was asked what party I belonged to I don't think I could say.'

The most experienced councillor is Mr F. G. E. Forsyth (Freddie to his friends). He could say what his politics are but won't. He was co-opted as an Independent after a spell in the wilderness: he had resigned from the council before when as chairman he had twice used his casting vote against 'a certain group' (the Labour councillors) and they accused him of partisanship. His political affiliation, he says, is his own affair and he doesn't like politics intruding into local government. He came to East Malling as a young man in 1932 to work at Ditton Laboratories, now part of East Malling Research Station but then a Government establishment. As a civil servant, albeit a scientific one, he had an added inducement to keep his politics to himself when he was first elected to the council in the mid-1930s. For the last forty years he has been on and off the council, mostly on; and although he has only returned to the council as a co-opted member since the last elections, his long experience made him a natural choice for vice-chairman when David Thornewell took George Holding's place.

Two of the Labour group who caused Freddie Forsyth's resignation were Mr and Mrs Arthur Gradwell. In the 1976 elections they were the sole successful Labour candidates (they were re-elected to district council as well). Since then this rump of the old Labour majority has resigned from the parish council in the face of a conclusive Liberal majority. Now, there are nine Liberals, five Independents, and Mr Michael Corcoran. Mr Corcoran is a burly, retiring Irishman who has lived in East Malling for thirteen years. He is a worker at the Kimberly Clark paper mill and, as he puts it, 'I'm a Conservative because although I'm only an ordinary working man I believe in free enterprise.' But though he stood as a Conservative he too feels that politics ought not to intrude into local government. His interest in the welfare of old folk led him to stand for the council in 1976, and it is in their interests that he is most often likely to interject a comment or a proposal in committee meetings.

If the sole Conservative is a surprise, the rest of the council are just as much of a mixed bag. Bernard Pollock is a Post Office engineer made redundant and now keeping body, soul, wife, family, Ford Consul and caravan, and a big house and garden together by working at Reed, where engineers are worth their weight in gold, though they are not paid it. He, too, is an anti-Labour Liberal, a chirpy South Londoner who had himself elected to the parish council because he felt that his end of the village — the houses strung out along the road to Wateringbury — wasn't represented. He thought it was time someone did something about the massive container lorries — the juggernaut menace, as the *Kent Messenger* dubbed the problem — roaring up the village High Street and along the Wateringbury Road. He lobbied and lobbied and eventually the Ministry of

Transport agreed to impose a width restriction. Bernie Pollock is what the Americans call a can-do man. He will take up anyone's cause and pester the life out of officialdom until he gets results. He prides himself on his diplomatic approach, but the outsider suspects that it is his sheer gadfly nuisance value that wins the day for him. He is one of the three district councillors, doesn't care for the formality of district council procedures, but puts in a hard stint there too (like travelling to Newcastle upon Tyne as one of a party to look at a sports complex and see whether it was the sort of thing that could be built in Larkfield).

The chairman, David Thornewell, is the councillor who makes it all tick over. It isn't so much that he is able to give off-the-cuff legal advice from time to time, though he does. It is his dedication. He is unmarried and gives most of his leisure to the parish council, the district council, and the Ramblers' Association (the announcements of the Sunday walks he fixes are one of the high spots of the parish paragraphs in the *Kent Messenger*). He is in his late thirties, so he is old enough to remember a lot of New Hythe before it was built on, and the water meadows and pasture land, and Larkfield Heath. It was watching the old Larkfield submerged willy-nilly that first moved him to stand for parish council.

'That's what really started it all off,' he says, 'and it becomes a bug, you know, once you get involved in it. I think the parish council work's very interesting. In fact I think it's more interesting than the district council. Because on the parish you've only got the clerk and that's the only admin-type officer there is. So if you want something done, or you've got a problem, then you've got to research it all out yourself, then go to the council and say now this is what we can do, and this is what I propose the council does. Whereas at the district council you say here's the problem and the officers go away and hopefully solve it or come back with a recommendation.'

Since 1972 David Thornewell has watched district council become more remote from people, but that has helped the parish council to become the real focus; that plus the 1972 statute that causes district to refer all planning applications to the parish for comment. And there have been successes. They stopped an old carpenter's shop in Mill Street from being turned into a light engineering works. Then there was the running fight over Anscombe's haulage business. The Anscombes are one of the families with roots in the village going back into the last century. They used to run the corn mill, but as mills became unprofitable they moved out with their horses and carts and started carrying parcels for villagers to Maidstone and London and back. In the years after the Second World War this had developed into a successful haulage business which now handles a fleet of trucks working on contract and moving containers between Kent and the Continent. Anscombes never had to have planning permission for their site beside the railway halt: by the time planning laws came in they were established users. But haulage is big business now and they consistently want to expand into the derelict orchard next door. So far the parish council has managed consistently to block their applications.

The council thought an application by a man who wanted to start a car-breaking business in Larkfield was dodgy on amenity grounds, and they successfully opposed that. And they went to the Public Inquiry over a wholesale furnishing firm with its offices in John Mercer's old oasts in Mill Street, which already had one large warehouse and wanted to build a second. There were objections from people living near the warehouse, basically on the grounds that traffic would increase and the balance between the residential and the business–industrial parts of the village would be upset. The council, with the Liberals and their news sheet *Hot-line* to the fore, took up the issue and cleverly focused opposition on the furnishing firm's proposals to run the historic mill stream and pond above the old corn mill through a concrete culvert. And on this ground the government inspector and the Minister upheld the objection.

But there are frustrations and defeats as well, and they are on the major issues. 'It's very difficult,' David Thornewell says. 'As a parish council we haven't got the resources to deal with those sort of applications very effectively. That is, developers come along and they've got counsel and solicitors and all the rest of it; and the parish council hasn't got enough money to match it really. We didn't want all those warehouses at the bottom of New Hythe Lane. Everyone agreed that there weren't going to be any warehouses. Therefore we left it to the county council to defend our case against the application at the Public Inquiry, and halfway through the Inquiry the county council's barrister decided to give in, saying that the county council had changed its mind. They actually changed their mind during the Inquiry! Of course the parish council wasn't represented and we lost out. I think this is the reverse side of having to do it all by yourself; by not having a planning staff, you can't cope with those sort of things.'

Then there was the time when parish council wishes were overridden by the parish at large — the last time, in fact, that there was a massive turnout for an annual parish meeting. The council wanted to build a village hall for East Malling and Larkfield parish. The parishioners from East Malling and Larkfield made it quite clear that they wanted one village hall for each ward, so the council reluctantly acquiesced — reluctantly because East Malling already had a village Institute hall. To make matters worse, the then Ministry of Transport was proposing to build the M 20 through New Hythe and hadn't settled on the line of the motorway. By the time they did, East Malling's village hall was built, four or five years had passed, and the costs of building had soared. But Larkfield got its village hall, just north of the motorway and a mile from East Malling's. There are problems: like the acoustics, which are so bad that when someone at the parish meeting proposes from the top table that something should be done to improve them nobody in the fourth row can hear what the proposal is. But by and large the halls are a success and it is clear that the parish was right to override its council; bookings are so heavy that one hall would never have been enough.

Inevitably a lot of the work of the council and its committees looks trivial, but it has to be done and it is done with dispatch. Mrs Wise complains at one meeting that the electrician who fitted the water heaters in East Malling village hall only had orange cable and it looks ugly where it emerges through a hole in the wall. 'Paint it,' the chairman proposes. Carried. The clerk tells the council that Larkfield Village Hall Committee is charging £6 rent for the old age pensioners' Christmas dinner. 'I don't want to twist your arms, but they are O.A.P.s,' he says, twisting arms. The chairman of the Village Hall Committee hadn't realised what was being done in his name and agrees to waive the charge. The Amenities Committee is worried about the amount of waste paper from Consolidated Paper Converters in New Hythe blowing around on a public footpath, and instructs the clerk to protest. An old lady has written to complain that the Maidstone bus company is taking a longer route from Larkfield to West Malling so that the fare is higher; and anyway the buses are irregular. The clerk agrees to write to the bus company and ask them to send an inspector to placate the old lady. At the next month's meeting Mr Terrell reports back that the bus company say the old lady has been rude to them in the past, but they will try to find an inspector to face the ordeal, and meanwhile they will work out an alteration to the route.

Time after time at council and committee meetings there is talk of fences: a fence to keep children from straying on to the embankment above the motorway, a fence to keep marauding children off the allotments; and when a parishioner complains about a Sunday football club sporadically booting their ball into his garden, the clerk reports back to his Allotments and Open Spaces Committee that he thinks the parishioner is hoping to take the council for the cost of a new fence. The old fence was there before the council bought the playing fields, the committee agree, and they let the complaint lie on file. And then there is the firm of spec builders putting up an estate in North Larkfield who appear, from the divergence between their plans and what is actually being built, to have mislaid twelve feet of land. If the council don't watch it, the committee say, the builders will have encroached on parish land. The council agree to watch it.

They are small enough matters, one by one: but one by one they add up to a burden of necessary work which, left undone, would make life in the village that much less tolerable. And fences and boundaries are the never-ending litany of local dispute. Here is a jury of the parish complaining:

> Also they present that Abraham Downing gent doth not keepe and make a sufficient fence against the footway leading from Abraham Ashedowne's orchard to the widow Evernden's garden and so along and they give him tyme to amend it before the ffeast of Christmas next uppon paine to forfeit to the Lord of the Mannor aforsaid 20 *d*.

That was the manor court meeting in 1658. Seven years earlier the same court decided that the newcomer Thomas Twisden was wrong in claiming two trees as part of his land: actually they belonged to James Peerson. And in 1794 the jury (which was called a homage and consisted of anything from eight to twelve manor tenants good and true) pronounced that 'John Larking Esqre hath erected two lodges on the Lord's wast at Warrens Green and that he hath stopped up a certain Ancient Watering place on the said heath and they recommend it to the Lord to enquire what damage has arisen to the tenants of the Manor by such Incroachments', which was an exact forerunner of the dispute that brought Mrs Lovering on to the parish council in 1978.

Before the Parliamentary Acts of 1888 and 1894 that created first county councils and then parish councils, the lords of the manor and the church had divided local administration between them. Even so, the ancient form of the manor court was derelict by the nineteenth century, and as early as the seventeenth was quite often only aping formula.

Every year it appointed aleconners to test the gravity of ale, and every year the aleconners reported back that they had been unable to fulfil the demands of their office because they had not been supplied with equipment. Every year, too, they appointed a reeve, the ancient office of tenants' representative to the lord and his steward. In 1652, when Sir John Rayney was still lord of the manor, the manor court appointed Thomas Twisden as reeve. In 1653 the homage entered in the court rolls: 'Thomas Twisden being chosen reeve at the last court here houlden by Francis Twisden Gent his brother appeared and requested the jury to set what ffyne they please uppon him for not performing that office of Reeve then the jury omitted to impose any ffyne but left it to the Lord.'

The benevolent forms of manor court and vestry were ill-equipped to deal with the agricultural and industrial revolutions; and what followed was too complex: unions of parishes administering the Poor Law of 1834, turnpike trusts administering the roads, charities administering schools (Holmes charity built one for East Malling in 1781), justices of the peace administering most other things through the medium of petty and quarter sessions. So county councils and rural district councils and parish councils were a needed rationalisation. At last country people had a say in their own local affairs.

But the reform of 1972 was from most points of view a step backwards. District council has become out of touch and more partisan. And the parish council in its most important activity, planning, is toothless. But it plugs away, its councillors are available, local, and in nobody's pocket, and it is a safeguard the community could not do without.

And if the parish council sometimes has the ground cut from under its feet because of its lack of professional backing, in other ways its amateurishness is its strength: it goes for the heart of the matter undeterred by finer nuances of the law. At a meeting of the Allotments and Open Spaces Committee the question arises of increasing the rent for allotments, maybe to £1.50 — again, because of the cost of fencing them. Bryn Terrell points out that the council last increased rents two years before. The current rent stands at 20 pence a rod, so a standard five-rod allotment costs £1.20 a year. One councillor remarks that other parishes have doubled, even trebled, their rents. Another reminds the committee that a lot of allotment holders are pensioners: perhaps they ought to be allowed half-rent? Pensioners don't like being treated as special cases, another councillor says.

Then David Thornewell weighs in with his legal knowledge. If the rent were to be raised above £1.25, he says, tenants could by law opt to pay the rent in quarterly instalments, which would be a nuisance to the clerk. Oh no, says Bryn Terrell, he has covered himself by drawing up an agreement which specifies that tenants should pay annually. Freddie Forsyth, who is in the chair in Bernie Pollock's absence through illness, agrees. That's what an annual tenant is, he says: if they pay quarterly, they won't be annual tenants, will they. Thornewell mildly quotes the Allotments Act, 1922, at the committee. 'We don't want to know about that,' someone remarks ungratefully. 'But you can't override an Act of Parliament with a contract,' Thornewell persists. 'Well I did,' Bryn Terrell snaps, and the committee agree that as far as they are concerned, the clerk's form of wording gets him off the hook. The committee decide to recommend to the full council a rent of 30 pence per rod, which makes it £1.50 for a full five-rod allotment. (Later, the full council will concur in this decision.)

It all amounts to an amazingly wrong-headed performance, but, in their infinite wisdom, they have come down on the side of common sense.

# 9 The future

**I tell you another thing I remember. You hear a lot about that English Channel tunnel don't you? They used to talk about that when I was at School.** Cecil John Chambers

*Robert Palmer's land from Walter's maps of the Twisden Estate*

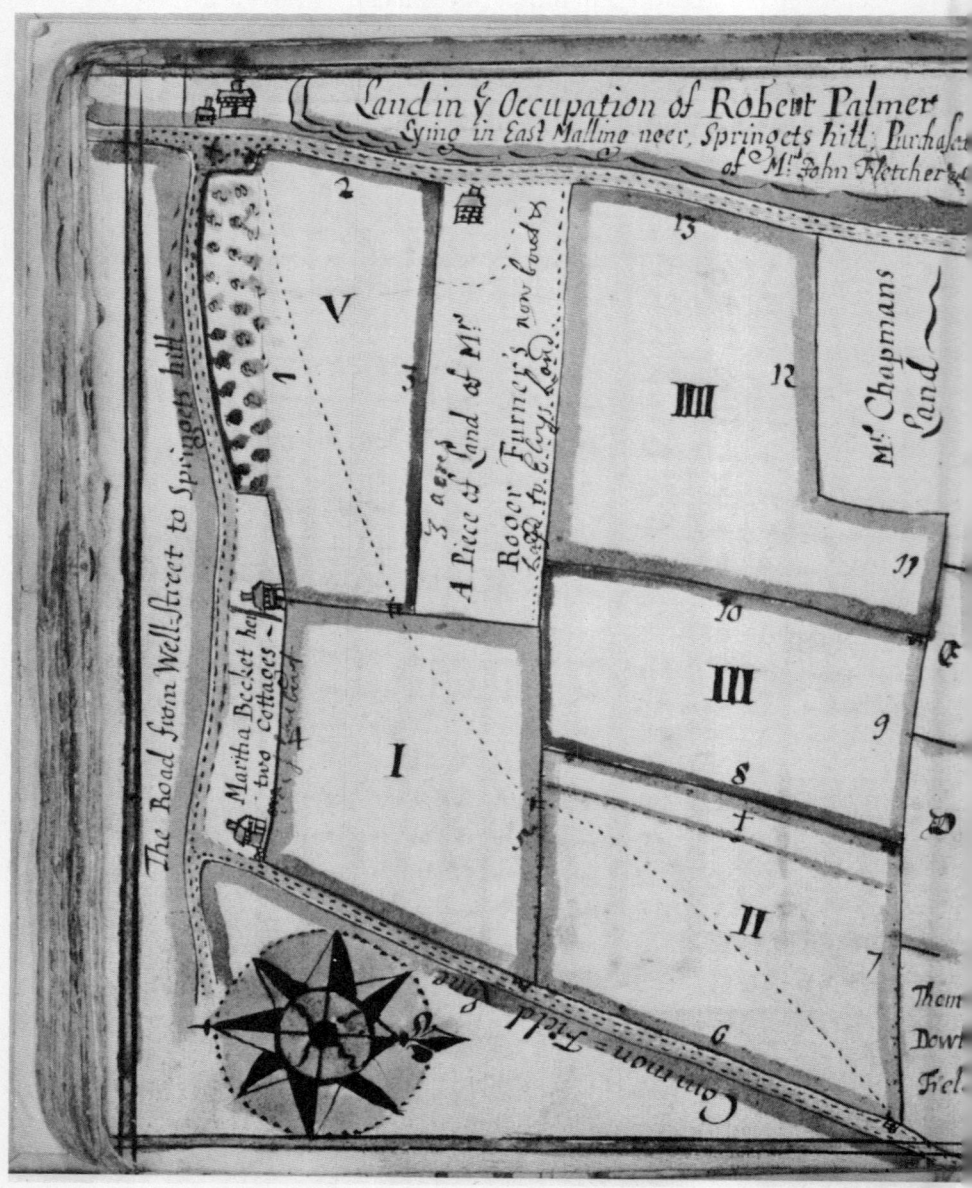

Time present and time past
Are both perhaps present in time future,
And time future contained in time past.     T. S. Eliot Four Quartets

## Names & Contents

| | | Ac: R: P: |
|---|---|---|
| I | Buke Field | 06 – 0 – 30 |
| II | Common=Field | 07 – 0 – 20 |
| III | Middle Field | 05 – 2 – 02 |
| IIII | Gun=Craft | 08 – 2 – 14 |
| V | Loam=herst hill | 07 – 1 – 15 |
| | Sum: of Acres | 34 – 3 – 01 |

### The Table of Timber

| | Elms | Pol Elm | Ash | Pol Ash |
|---|---|---|---|---|
| 1 | 59 | 56 | 16 | – |
| 2 | 4 | 3 | – | 5 |
| 3 | – | – | – | 4 |
| 4 | – | – | – | 20 |
| 5 | – | 2 | – | 11 |
| 6 | – | – | – | 3 |
| 7 | – | – | – | 2 |
| 8 | – | – | – | 6 |
| 9 | – | 7 | – | 9 |
| 10 | – | 5 | 6 | – |
| 11 | – | 20 | 4 | – |
| 12 | – | 30 | 4 | 3 |
| 13 | – | 5 | – | – |
| | 130 | 75 | 19 | 60 |

| | |
|---|---|
| Ellms | 130 |
| Pol: Elm | 75 |
| Ashes – | 79 |
| | 284 |

Note that Commonfield Lane
is part of the premises & was formerly
hedged off from the said Land, by the
Owner for his owne conveniency &c.
Within the Prickt Line where this (†)
mark Standeth is an Acre of Land
which belongs to the Vicarege of
East Malling (: where this (+) mark
Standeth is called Springets hill
& is in the Road which leadeth
from Broadwater to Crouch green

IF THE RAGSTONE church is the heart of the village, its arteries run right through the old East Malling. Ragstone is everywhere. It was easier and cheaper to build houses in wattle and daub and timber, and later to clad some of those buildings in brick and tile, but there are ragstone walls down New Road and Clare Lane, in fields, in kitchen gardens, along Mill Street, and up the high ground by Paris Farm. Beneath the railway bridge in the bosky depths of Stickens Lane the road level has sunk so deep that the ragstone and hassock of the Hythe beds are as naked as a quarry face. West Malling is all Georgian elegance, red, orange, purple brick, white sash and door post such as East Malling can only aspire to in its masterpiece, Bradbourne. People who grew up in East Malling remember it as the grey stone village, grey, grey walls hanging over their heads as they made their way to grey school.

But description is a thankless drab. In twilight, lichen turns grey into green and shadowed indigo. In sunshine the church takes on, a little, the honey glow of Cotswold stone. In rain, the ragstone is so saturated it weeps. It is so easily quarried, and the Medway wharves so accessible to the Thames, that the Romans used ragstone to build their wall around London, and Gundulf built his towers and churches with it, and the younger Cundy and the older Scott and Butterfield and Poynter built their neo-Gothic in Pimlico with it. But ragstone and soot sit uneasily together and godly Victorian piety turned glum in the smoke. And to the builder who looks for fine effects, ragstone is as coarse as the volcanic rock of Cumbria.

The genius of Kent is brick and tile; the genius of East Malling is ragstone. That, and hawthorn. Hawthorn here is what dry-stone walls are in the north, but more impenetrable. The history of the village can be told in its hedges and lanes and footpaths. There are hedges that go back to the foundation of the Abbey in 1090, and there are footpaths that go in a scarcely deviating line from East Malling and from Broadwater to the Abbey through the hedges. There are hedges that date back between four and five hundred years — at a guess, to the redistribution of land after the dissolution — and there are hedges that go back to enclosure. There is New Hythe Lane, the lifeline to the wharf that became so muddy across the marsh land that the parish overseer put the gangs of unemployed farm labourers on to it to earn their Speenhamland pittance. Then there is the London road over the Heath, which peters out now into gorse and bramble at the end of the airfield runway, and the new London road (the military way of the Saxon document) which meandered around the tiny court house in the middle of Larkfield Green, at the crossroads, until the coming of the toll roads and the stage and waggon traffic to London.

You can even read Domesday in the face of the landscape of this anciently manorial and anciently enclosed village. For if you take Brad-bourne, with its Old English name (brad/burna: practically a synonym for Broadwater) and its classic geographical position in relation to the church, and if you look at the natural boundaries, Winterfield Lane, the London Road, Mill Street, the churchyard, and the eastern boundary which is held in common with the parish, and allowing for sales and pur-chases and knocking off parcels of land for common fields and villein tenants — whatever combination of these you still come up with three hundred acres, give or take. And three hundred acres is near enough the two sulings of the demesne farm outlined in the Domesday Book entry for Metlinges (East Malling).

'Instead of trundling the theodolite,' Sir Francis Palgrave wrote of the Norman and Saxon farmers, 'they yoked the oxen and sped the plough.' In other words, they measured land by the amount of work a team of oxen could get through in a year, and the ground is thick with Domesday scholars who have tried to arrive at an interpretation. But there is a con-sensus view, and the evidence here adds up to Bradbourne.

Finding the thirty-eight villein farms would be the real trick. Broad-water, certainly. Springate Farm, Cobb Hall, Gig Hill, Little Lunsford, Great Lunsford: some or all of these. The Barracks in Well Street, a big handsome house with projecting solar wing and barge-boards carved with owls at the gable apex. The Derbies opposite, with its medieval window frames. Springhead Farm. Due east of that, the big farmhouse on Chapel Street singled out in print by Arthur Mee, no longer a farm but the home of an actor who grew to maturity in the service of *The Mousetrap* in the West End of London. The small Wealden hall house in Church Walk. Holm House in the High Street, now the vicarage, and Cecil John Chambers's house opposite, disguised by stucco, timber and brick and barnyard behind.

Halfway down Mill Street is a group of four cottages arranged in three sides of a square, brick and tile: a yeoman's seventeenth-century long-house in disguise. For behind the brick of the two cottages in the centre is the timber frame — the prefabrication of its day — and the wattle and daub infill. By 1750 the tenant of Upper Mill lived there, a man called James Brooks. And maybe it was James Brooks who built in the fashion-able new cased sash windows. In 1803 James Brooks (or his son) was still there. He died that year and his wife Margaret Brooks kept on the mill for another year until John Larking took over. By 1810 James Thornhill had moved into the longhouse. He was a yeoman who had taken up the expanding new trade of plumbing, and that with glazing and decorating were to make him a rich man, with a family tomb in the churchyard and a small stained-glass window in the south aisle. Half-timbered houses were distinctly out of fashion, and he converted this one by cladding the upper floor with tile and disguising the overhang by a frontage of brick for the ground floor. Then he added to the rudely trimmed roof beams a superstructure — not wooden dowelled now but hammered together with long nails from the smithy in the High Street — and raised the pitch of the roof at the rear to create out of the attic space three extra bedchambers. And at right angles to the front of the house he added two more cottages: one he rented out, to the other he added a bow window and a board above painted with his name and trade.

Further down the street, there is the misnamed Clare Cottage, a big rambling house sixteenth or seventeenth century at the core. Then a half-timbered cottage with an overhang, divided into two now but once perhaps a small farmhouse, though by 1679 it was the cottage of Edmund Gilder, a linen weaver. Abraham Walter was not only the Twisdens' surveyor and a church warden when the first five bells were founded and hung in 1695 (his name is inscribed on the tenor bell); he also farmed by copyhold from the lord 26 acres 12 perches of land by the corner of New Hythe Lane and Larkfield Green. Still, when he died in 1715 he was so heavily in debt that his will was simply a list of instructions for the sale of his property, including 'all that land known as Chalk Croft in East Malling', to pay off his creditors. The house next to the former Bull Inn is almost all that remains of the old Larkfield.

The evidence for the Domesday village is there in the surviving buildings and in the archive records of the vanished buildings, in the long-gone names of the copyhold families, passing on their homes to their descendants but paying a herriot to the lord of the manor and renewing their fealty. A scholar with time to spare could make an educated guess at the whereabouts of those thirty-eight villein farms of 1086. And it matters. The great rebuilding of Elizabethan times never matched anything that has happened in our own day; the Parliamentary Enclosure of the Heath and the clearing of a new farm from the woods was nothing like the revolution of the railway and the car and the London worker driven to commuting by prices and the need to escape from life in a polyglot city of millions. So it matters that the old Larkfield and New Hythe have been annihilated and that Aylesford, once one of the loveliest of

England's villages, has one of the unloveliest industrial estates on her doorstep. It matters that we should learn the lesson. For when David Thornewell's parish council was trodden underfoot as county council government contrived with industry to build more massive warehouses in New Hythe, it was the victim of a broad policy decision that rode roughshod over local opinion; and beyond that policy-making forum there is national government, and beyond that, if the idealists, as they think of themselves, have their way, there will be Europe, shaping industries and changing landscapes. So local knowledge and opinion matter more and more and are in danger of being more and more neglected.

To be fair to the county council, it has produced a document called the Kent Structure Plan which is designed to see the county through to the 1990s without any more of the depredations that have scarred the lower reaches of the Medway valley. The plan is an intellectually and professionally formidable attempt to reconcile the irreconcilable: the need to conserve and the need to build more houses and create more jobs for the newcomers. It is sensitive to the needs of the separate areas, not just those that retain their appeal as part of the garden of England, but those that have already been spoiled. And yet the danger is, that while it preserves agriculture and industry working side by side as they always have in England's oldest civilised county, it will turn villages into museums for car-borne commuters to live in and car-borne tourists to visit. A map with stippled green dots signifying 'Areas of special significance for countryside conservation' does not show how the heart has been ripped out of a village like Wrotham by a motorway interchange. Here every field and its history could be — indeed, has been — traced back to pre-Reformation days. Here was the strip field where Thomas Twisden bought out some of the villagers, and where one of the encounters of the Civil War was fought: was, because it is lost now under the motorway. Ancient footpaths have gone forever, ancient hedgebanks and rows of trees uprooted. If you think none of this matters, talk to the villagers. What is left is a Wrotham cut off from its past by everyone else's hurrying present. But the village has been preserved, and if you choose your camera angle carefully, it makes a charming snap.

Then take an example closer to home. In East Malling in the late 1830s and early '40s John Styles and John Akehurst each had a baker's shop, Thomas Godfrey and Isaac Pemble each had a butcher's shop. James Yeomans was the carpenter at the west end of Mill Street and John Larking (another John Larking) at the top of High Street. George Blunden was the landlord of the King and Queen and Lydia Jessup of the Ship. They were the only two pubs at the time (compared with seven in the memory of Cecil John Chambers), but there were five beer shops as well, taking advantage of the abolition of the tax on beer by the Duke of Wellington's Beer House Act. That became law on 12 October 1830 when, as the *Maidstone Journal* reported, 'all the breweries in the kingdom exhibited a scene of almost unprecedented bustle and activity.' Anyone could sell beer from his parlour on payment of a small fee, and Charlotte Church, George Letchford, Thomas King, Thomas Webb, and Richard Fry bought licences in East Malling. Richard Fry started a line of business which stuck: today his house is the Rising Sun pub. John Waggon was the saddler and harness maker. George and Sarah Edmett, William Hall, and George Richardson were all grocers, James Thornhill the plumber, painter, and glazier, Nicholas Ongley the tailor, John Hubble the wheelwright, Henry and George Letchford the blacksmiths, Richard Courts and Douglas Jones boot and shoe makers. By 1847 there were four boot and shoe makers, and one of them, James Huggett, doubled as a watch and clock repairer.

No one in the hypermarket society could reasonably expect all those kinds of shops to survive in a small village. Ford Cortinas don't need a wheelwright or a blacksmith. There are a couple of grocers still, and a newsagent-cum-post-office-cum-stationers, an antique shop and a guest house, and two of the old trades, a butcher and a baker.

Basil Tompsett is the butcher. His shop and home is the cottage handed down from Thomas Godfrey through Jabez John Chambers. It still has the iron rail outside for hanging the turkeys from at Christmas (you don't do that now if you don't want to lose them). He still, like most old family butchers, makes his own sausages from his unique recipe. He still sports a straw boater which he tips to customers as they pass by the shop.

His grandfather was a butcher, with a shop in Penshurst. His father was a butcher. Both his sons are butchers: one has a business in the shopping square in Larkfield, the other has two shops, at Rainham and Chatham, and when it comes to meat he is the voice of Radio Medway. Basil Tompsett started in the trade aged fifteen, apprenticed to his uncle.

He doesn't do his own slaughtering any more because he is on his own; if you get a bad animal when you are by yourself it can be very tricky. He remembers his first killing. He had only been in the trade two or three weeks when he was given a bullock to pole-axe. Fifth of November 1927, it was. He kept the horns a long time, stamped with the date. Doesn't know what's become of them now. A pole-axe was like a normal axe except that on the other side of the shaft from the blade was a hollow spike, very sharp. You had to hit the bullock between the eyes with the spike, pull it out, and push a bit of straw in the hole. It was a quick death all right, but, of course, you had to learn. Basil Tompsett reckoned himself lucky with that kill: he knew as soon as he started in the business that sooner or later he would have to do it so he used to practise on logs.

That went out in about 1932 or 1933, he can't quite remember when, but he remembers he was glad. It was a gory business. The captive bolt came in, and pole-axing was outlawed. The captive bolt is attached to a small pistol. You load the pistol with a blank and when you fire it the bolt goes through the bullock's skull and a greased suction pad retracts it into the barrel. Basil Tompsett was particularly glad they didn't any longer have to kill a calf by tapping it on the side of the head with the flat of the axe blade to stun it, then slit its throat and hang it up by the hind legs. And in his day, he stuck hundreds of sheep and pigs, slitting down the throat — 'slitting across is koshering, the Jewish way: they even do it to chickens.' It was gory, all right.

Basil Tompsett is pensionable now, but says he couldn't give it up and do nothing. Mr A. G. Steel-Clark could, and means to. He is the baker and he has been working towards retirement in a bungalow at Herne Bay since 1936. His first job was in London, then up on the North Downs at Meopham, then in Gravesend, always for big bakery firms. Ten years ago he had saved enough to pay half down on the shop with bakery adjoining in East Malling. He cannot remember what it is like to work in the daytime. He and Mrs Clark have never had a holiday. When they take a break, it is to do maintenance work on the house and the bakery. When he was a young man in the trade he had a colleague who had never taken a holiday and he told himself that he would never get caught on the same treadmill. He has, but when he gets that bungalow his first aim is to take a very long holiday with his wife touring Britain in a caravanette. Mr Clark's brother works for BL motors at Cowley and makes a good wage with a forty-hour week, and he thinks Mr Clark is barmy to live the life he does. But as a master baker he is at no one's beck and call, and though it looks like back-breaking work he wouldn't have it any other way. In any case, he says, he has no intention of breaking his back (actually, he has slipped a disc but it only bothers him when he is doing nothing, so that's all right). He works by choice without an assistant and is saving a nest egg big enough to retire on but not enough for the tax man to bite too deeply. His wife opens the shop at 8 a.m. and it's a slow day if with the help of an assistant she hasn't cleared the shelves by ten o'clock.

Working alone in the bakery, four hundred pounds of dough will give Mr Clark a couple of hundred assorted loaves: white, Hovis, wheatmeal, Danish, bloomers, cottage loaves, farmhouse, mixed smalls, round loaves, rectangular loaves, loaves split down the middle or slashed a dozen times diagonally across the crust, glossy loaves, matt loaves; will also make Eccles cakes, fruit tarts, and an assortment of buns: ordinary buns and cream buns and sticky buns.

Normally he starts work at one o'clock in the morning. On Fridays and bank holidays he puts in overtime, starting at 10 p.m., sometimes with one of his married daughters helping to carry trays of bread and dough about. The temperature in the ovens rises to about 500° Fahrenheit and in the white-tiled bakery to about 74°, so Mr Clark is light-clad for work: a white T-shirt, light cotton khaki trousers hitched up beneath a brown leather belt, tennis shoes without laces. He is a wiry man with shoulder-blades sticking out through the T-shirt like dorsal fins, but with broad shoulders from years of kneading and heaving sacks of flour.

He begins work by preparing the dough. When he was starting in the trade, he says, the golden rule was twice as much water as flour. Now to the two seventy-pound bags of flour, Rank's Bakers Pride, he adds thirty-four quarts of water, eight gallons. Plus a pound and a half of yeast, the same of lard, three-quarters of a pound of sugar, and seventeen ounces of salt: half an ounce of salt for every quart of water; the salt stabilises the yeast, and if you cut the salt down the process is faster but the bread isn't as good.

These materials go into a machine that looks like a fair-sized concrete mixer. Even in a small family business, there is a lot of labour-saving machinery, though Mr Clark disapproves of too much: it 'fells' the dough, he says; 'ruptures the cells, I suppose. Anyway, it doesn't rise so well.' The simplest bakery he has ever seen, and the one with the most beautiful bread, was a one-man show in Surrey, with brick-built, wood-fired ovens. It had bare brick walls as well and an earthen floor, so 'they' closed it down.

Mr Clark's own ovens are fired by oil. When he came to East Malling the ovens lived on coke but he had them converted seven years ago. At the time, they consumed £28 worth of oil a month; now the same oil costs £180 but the saving in labour is enormous. As it is, it is difficult to see how stoking up coke-fired ovens would fit into the routine. Once he has started kneading dough he will not stop moving for nearly seven hours, until the last batch of bread is baking and the shop is about to open. At 5.30 Mrs Clark, in dressing gown and hairnet, brings him a big china mug of tea and two hot buttered rolls, but tea and rolls are cold before he consumes them. Mrs Clark is up at five every morning, she says. Except, he says drily, on Sunday: then she lies in until six.

When the dough is ready, he carries heavy armfuls of it across to a Formica-topped work bench. He takes a sharp butcher's knife and chops off two-pound chunks, checks the weight on old-fashioned kitchen scales, and drops the chunks one by one into a machine labelled Mono Universal; out they tumble at the bottom shaped into loaves. Within half a minute he has a dozen. Shaping by hand, as he deftly demonstrates, would take ten times as long. Another skill that will be lost; more time gained, more effort saved. Who's complaining, even if the bakery schools are feeding fewer notable characters into the new, streamlined trade? After the war, Mr Clark had hired himself out at a shilling and a farthing an hour standing at a bench shaping bloomers, or victory loaves as they became known at the time. Maybe that, he concedes, is what it would feel like to work on a conveyor belt for British Leyland.

The first batch of buns and loaves is ready for the oven. Once the dough would be made from U.S., Canadian, or Australian wheat, which was cheaper and harder. Now EEC regulations insist that bakers must use soft French wheat; expensive and not as good for baking, though all right for the big bakeries. 'But then, they could make bread out of chalk and water.' Once, Mr Clark used New Zealand apples for his pies. Now he must use tinned apples from Italy and in each expensive two-kilo tin is a pint of water with the apples. Before, he used cheap powdered milk from New Zealand in the dough. Now he must use powdered milk from the Continent, or do without. He does without.

He feeds the loaves in their separate tins into the oven with a long paddle known in the trade as a peel. The open oven doors send a warm blast of air heated to 450° Fahrenheit into the bakery. Mr Clark pushes the doors to. The rolls will be ready in fifteen minutes, the buns in eight minutes, the loaves in forty. He doesn't make as high a proportion of buns as he used to: chips play a bigger part in people's diet now. As for bread as a whole, well, factory-produced sliced loaves are very convenient, and it has got so that some people actually prefer the taste of damp blotting paper. But when there is a strike at the major bakeries and the queues straggle up under the railway bridge waiting for Mr Clark's bread, there are always plenty of compliments for him. Like water off a duck's back, he says.

With one lot baking in the oven, there is the next lot to prepare: to shape, to slash diagonally or straight down the middle — stops the loaves bursting in the oven. There are the black currant pies to make. He likes to put in a generous filling, but today he overdoes it and when the pies come out of the oven they stick to the baking tray, which makes work he could do without.

One batch of loaves comes out, another batch of three dozen goes in. Meanwhile he prepares the buns, brushing on a light coating of simple syrup from an old can to make the sticky buns sticky. Once he experimented with a patent mixture, but it wasn't sticky and the customers didn't like it. So he went back to his mixture of sugar and water: fondant if he is in a hurry.

By now it is 6.45 and Mrs Clark is here to start moving trays of bread through to the shop across the narrow alley. There are numbers of heavy wooden trays but another breakthrough was the acquisition of wire trays that stack into a tall trolley on wheels: easier to move, and they need no shelf space. By now Mr Clark is flattening out pie dough and folding it over, flattening and folding, flattening and folding. The theory is that the layers of fat stop the water escaping so the pastry flakes. 'Some people can make it, some people can't. Some days it's good, some days it's not so good.' Most of his views are thrown off this cryptically, maybe because he is used to being alone through the dawn with Radio Medway (at 6.15 he switches to Radio Four: it tells you what the farmers are doing, he says, and how happy they are at all the money they are making).

Next comes a batch of buns to have white icing sugar coated on the tops. A couple of dozen done in no time, and one removed from the batch for a cherry to be added plumb centre. 'Special order; my grandson.' The next lot he slits down the side, then squeezes cream into them from the sort of bag-and-nozzle affair that housewives use to decorate cakes. In the trade it is called a savoy, pronounced 'savvy'. Half these buns get a chocolate top, half are sprinkled with icing sugar. The second batch gets a glacé cherry each — or rather, half a cherry. Mr Clark makes the cans of cherries go further since the price went up, but they are French and good; and a good size too. That lot of buns finished, he puts them on a tray, regards them sceptically, and remarks: 'There's sugar in the mix, sugar in the filling, and sugar in the topping. People on a diet say, well, one bun won't hurt. Put on half a stone straight away.'

By now it is quarter to eight. For the first time he pauses in his travels between dough-making machine, work bench, and oven, and fills a pipe.

For the past four years there was always a sparrow that would sit on the window sill outside and watch him work. This year it hasn't come back and Mr Clark does the watching: a pair of wrens nesting in a shrub by the house and bringing up their young. The egg-timer that punctuates the night with shrill reminders rings again. Bloomers and Danish loaves ready to come out of the oven. Eight o'clock, shop's open. Mr Clark starts cleaning up. The last loaves are baking. Eight-thirty: another day's work drawing to a close.

East Malling is lucky. Mr Clark has found another baker to buy his business as a going concern. The village could be lucky again when Mr Tompsett finally hangs up his straw boater but the odds are against. Everywhere, the small butcher is closing down in the face of competition from supermarkets. 'I think there are only three small butcher's shops in Maidstone,' Basil Tompsett says, 'and look at the size of that town. Eighteen years ago there were six of us in this shop, including my two sons and Mary full time on the cash desk. Now, just me, Mary part time, and a girl to help with delivering on Saturdays.'

In its Structure Plan, the county council accepts as an accomplished fact that the Medway villages have been despoiled. It doesn't name the villages but lumps them together as the Medway Gap, thus tacitly condemning them to life as an unlovely conurbation. And who can blame the council? If you stand in the churchyard of Holy Trinity among the tombstones already weathered and yew trees darker than sleep and the neatly trimmed sward, it seems God's little acre. But over the ragstone wall there is nothing but warehouses and mills, acre upon acre of industrial desolation stretching across to Aylesford. Down there where Pepys saw the river twist and turn so mightily the occasional seagoing steamer still moves slowly through the meadows and between the two towered churches of Burham and Snodland. But the hinterland is all housing estates, industrial estates, and roads planned to siphon the big lorries as fast as possible on to the motorway. Incongruously in the middle of this is a little lake that has been made a nature conservancy. And all this is the area which the planners have looked at and declared, with that shining unshakeable optimism that characterises the breed in the face of the multiple untidiness and unpredictability of real life, that a district centre — meaning offices and shops — will be the heart that pumps life into this amorphous area and turns it into a community. Now all this recognises that the Government has designated the Medway Gap a growth point, that people are moving into Kent whether Kent wants them or not and it is right that they should have the choice, that to the west and south of the Medway Gap are villages and countryside that must be preserved, and that Maidstone as a shopping centre is already crowded. And, of course, public transport is a dirty word.

So operating within these restrictions the Kent plan is good: except that a shopping centre with a huge supermarket, which is what the planners envisage, will scorch the earth round about. It is regarded as visionary impracticality — and it is certainly politically unfashionable — to suggest that money should be spent on subsidising corner shops in the new neighbourhoods so that the small butcher, the baker, the grocer, the family-run news agency can be revived. Yet it would cost a fraction of the money now spent on the roads programme. The road builder is king. And in County Hall and beyond the friends who own supermarket chains, the big spenders, carry more weight than local opinion even where local opinion manifests itself as it did when Leybourne was first named as the site for the new district centre. County Hall isn't corrupt, it is remote and subject to different pressures from the pressures imposed on parish councillors. And current County Hall and Government policies mean that, with luck and continuing goodwill, the villages will be preserved all right, as dormitories and tourist sights. Kent grew up as the mediator between the Continent and the rest of the kingdom, as London's market garden and orchard, as the founder of the cannons that won the Battle of Trafalgar. But now for the first time, and especially when the Germans and French build the Channel Tunnel for us, it is in danger of losing its own life and integrity and becoming no more than the sum of the picture postcard views.

# Index

Places named are within the parish of East Malling and Larkfield
unless otherwise indicated.